The Festive Teacher

The Festive Teacher

Multicultural Activities for Your Curriculum

Steve Springer, Brandy Alexander, and Kimberly Persiani-Becker, Ed.D.

New York   Chicago   San Francisco   Lisbon   London   Madrid   Mexico City
Milan   New Delhi   San Juan   Seoul   Singapore   Sydney   Toronto

Contents

Introduction

The *Festive Teacher* has been developed as a resource for new and veteran teachers in need of academic and curricular ideas for addressing and teaching holidays. While there are many books out there today that offer wonderfully creative activities for each of the major holidays recognized by the majority of people today, our book does that and more. The holidays included here have been chosen because they are important historically, culturally, and even religiously in some cases. More than that, holidays in this book span to various countries outside the United States. In addition, several holidays that are celebrated in countries other than the United States have also been included. This offers an opportunity for your students to be exposed to celebrations in other parts of the world.

Each holiday begins with a short historical explanation. This is especially important for those teachers who only have a personal experience with the date and don't have much background to share with students. The explanations have been researched to check facts and then have been truncated to provide a non-overwhelming picture for teachers to share with their students. As with most of the holidays addressed in this book, it is important that teachers encourage students to do their own research on the holidays or even assign a research report if teachers want their students to get a detailed account of the traditions, history, and cultural perspective. You will find some suggestions listed under "Lesson Extensions" on the Teacher Resource Page, which is the last section of each holiday.

After a brief history of each holiday, teachers will find activity pages and journal pages available to help students connect the holiday to curricular areas. At a time when academics are at the forefront of practice in the classroom today, we wanted teachers to be able to include the holidays into their curricular areas without feeling the need to "justify" including the holidays into the standards. The activity pages provide students with key words and/or vocabulary, math questions, and holiday activities. Along with the activity pages, there are holiday journal pages. These journal pages give students the opportunity to write and/or illustrate something about each holiday.

Once the teacher has used the grade-level activity sheets and journal pages for the holiday, there are art activities that follow. These are great for bulletin boards, and they are fun for the students.

The last section for each holiday is a Teacher Resource Page. This is where teachers will find bulletin board ideas that address all the district criteria needed to set up a complete bulletin board. There is also a list of extension activities to keep the academic component engaged. This is followed by a Word Bank of key words that teachers might want to use for spelling, writing, or vocabulary. Finally, there is a list of relevant children's books, both fiction and nonfiction. These books serve as wonderful read-alouds, research resources, and shared reading or silent reading experiences. Some also include additional art activities.

In creating this book, we pulled many of the activities we have done with our own students through the years. We also looked at websites and children's picture books. Additionally we spoke with several other teachers who shared their ideas and historical perspectives based on their own personal experiences celebrating these holidays throughout their lives. When a holiday was new to us, we engaged in conversations with friends and family members from various parts of the world who were willing to read what we found out about each holiday and give their feedback. With this, we were able to make holiday descriptions more current and shed less relevant information. The end result is a brief but complete background of each holiday. With this in mind, once again, we remind you to have students research holidays for more detailed time lines, for a more in-depth look at historical figures, and to compare and contrast holidays across cultural lines.

We hope you enjoy *The Festive Teacher*. The intent of this book was not to just offer simple art activities for students and teachers, but to also encourage students and teachers to study more about the background of each holiday as a way to eliminate the commercialism often related to holidays today. We have had great fun developing it. We have learned a lot not only about the holidays new to us, but also about holidays we have been celebrating all our lives.

Acknowledgments

We dedicate *The Festive Teacher* to Kathryn Keil, our editor at McGraw-Hill. Her devotion to our work and our vision is why we have been able to produce the teacher resource books we have always wanted to share with new and veteran teachers. Kathryn stands behind our proposals and gets others to become as excited about our potential books as we are. Thank you, Kathryn, for your support and dedication in helping us to provide exciting and necessary resources to teachers in classrooms today.

Dr. Martin Luther King Jr.'s Birthday

Dr. Martin Luther King was a minister, a political activist, and one of the most important historical figures in the American civil rights movement. He is remembered worldwide for his work on racial equality and nonviolent change. Born in Atlanta, Georgia, on January 15, 1929, the son of a schoolteacher and a Baptist minister, he was taught throughout his life that all people need to be treated with respect. His father's ministry included efforts to break down race barriers and to increase voting among African Americans.

But from an early age Martin saw how people were often judged and treated differently because of the color of their skin. From water fountains to public buses to schools, segregation of blacks from whites was rampant in the American South during this time. Even Martin's white childhood friend was not allowed to play with him once the friend started attending a school only for whites.

Young Martin, or ML as his family called him, was smart, learning to read even before he went to school. He was an outstanding student and skipped grades in elementary and high school, entering college when he was just 15 years old. He graduated from Morehouse College at age 19 and then followed his father's footsteps, receiving a degree from Crozer

Theological Seminary. He later went on to earn his Ph.D. in theology from Boston University. While in school, he studied the philosophies of Mahatma Gandhi and the peaceful revolution Gandhi led to free the people of India from British rule. This influenced Martin greatly, and he would later imitate these philosophies to fight the inequalities and segregation that African Americans faced in the United States.

While in college, Martin married music student Coretta Scott, and they moved to Montgomery, Alabama. They later had four children. In 1953, Martin became the pastor of the Dexter Avenue Baptist Church and began his ministry. But unrest between the black and white citizens of Montgomery was becoming hard to ignore, and on December 1, 1955, a woman named Rosa Parks refused to give up her seat to a white person on the segregated bus. Rosa was arrested, and the American civil rights movement was born. Dr. King (with other African American leaders) led a protest in the form of a boycott of the Montgomery bus system. For 382 days, African Americans and white people who supported them refused to ride the buses, essentially bankrupting the Montgomery public transit system. With this form of nonviolent protest, Martin would set the stage for other victories against discrimination, and he went on to become one of the primary forces of the civil rights movement.

Much of the rest of Dr. King's life was marked with marches, sit-ins, boycotts, and court battles. On August 28, 1963, Dr. King delivered his most famous speech, the I Have a Dream speech, on the steps of the Lincoln Memorial in Washington, D.C. This speech embodied all that Dr. King believed in and is regarded as one of the finest speeches in U.S. history. In 1964, Dr. King's leadership and contributions to the civil rights movement earned him the Nobel Peace Prize.

Tragically, Dr. King was assassinated on April 4, 1968, in Memphis, Tennessee. But his contributions were not forgotten. In 1983, President Ronald Reagan signed a bill creating a federal holiday to honor him and his legacy. The holiday was observed for the first time in 1986, and since 2000 has been celebrated in all 50 states on the third Monday in January, the month in which Dr. King was born.

Name: _____ Date: _____

assassinated	equality	leader	judged	character
race	dream	African American	civil rights	demonstration

Illustrate these four words:

dream   equal   leader   bus

A city bus picked up 4 people when it stopped for the first time. At a second stop, 6 more people get on. At a third stop, 3 more people got on the bus. How many people in all got on the bus? Show your work.

Which person is Dr. Martin Luther King Jr.? Circle him.

Where do dreams happen? Circle the answer.

Make a list of 5 things you have dreamed about.

1. _____
2. _____
3. _____
4. _____
5. _____

Draw yourself asleep in the bed. Draw a picture of your dream of helping someone do something good!

Name: _____ Date: _____

Illustrate these four words:

dream	*leader*	*demonstration*	*minister*

If you have 6 buses, and 5 people get on each bus, how many people in total are on the buses? Draw people on the buses using X's. There are _____ people.

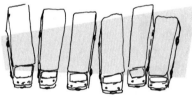

Dr. King loved to read. Cross out the item he would *not* have been able to read. Draw one other item you can read.

Dr. King was born on Jan. 15, 1929, in Atlanta, Georgia. Where and when were you born?

Month and Day _____

Year _____

City _____

State _____

Country _____

How many years after Dr. King was born were you born?

_____ years _____ months

Dr. King was helpful to all people, and believed in equality, especially for people unable to help themselves. Draw a picture of yourself doing something nice or helpful for another.

Dr. King had a dream that one day all boys and girls would hold hands and come together as friends. Draw in the missing children and the background. Write about why your friends are important to you.

_____

_____

_____

_____

_____

_____

_____

_____

_____

_____

_____

_____

Name:

Date:

Below is a picture of the house Dr. King lived in. In the other box, draw a picture of the home you live in now. When you're finished drawing your home, write about the things that are similar between the two homes and the things that are different. Color both pictures when you're finished.

Name: _____ Date: _____

All of these children are doing helpful things for other people. Explain what is happening in the pictures. Dr. King would be proud to see people helping one another.

_____

_____

_____

_____

_____

_____

_____

_____

_____

_____

_____

_____

_____

_____

_____

_____

Name: _____ Date: _____

Make a list of three things you can do today to improve or help the world! Good luck, and remember, with your help the world can be a better place to live.

1. _____

_____

_____

_____

2. _____

_____

_____

_____

3. _____

_____

_____

_____

Write about equality and why it is important to lend a helping hand to people regardless of their race, nationality, or beliefs. Illustrate.

_____

_____

_____

_____

_____

_____

_____

_____

_____

_____

_____

_____

_____

Dr. King's Birthday Triptych Pyramid

Students can create a triptych pyramid for any theme that you choose. In the spirit of Dr. King, students can draw a picture in each triangle of a dream they have had, or something positive they have done.

Follow the directions below, and students can use these pyramids as great motivation for their writing.

Materials

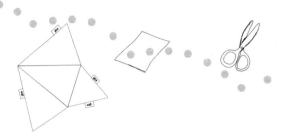

triptych template
paper
crayons
glue
scissors

1. Cut out the pyramid template on the following page.

2. Color a different picture on each triangle; these can be theme-based or entirely arbitrary, depending on instructions.

3. After drawing and coloring the pictures, fold the triangles to form a pyramid.

4. Fold tabs to the inside and put a little glue on each tab. Hold the pyramid together until dry.

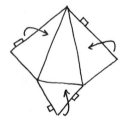

5. When finished, students can choose one side of the pyramid to write about, or discuss their pictures with a neighbor.

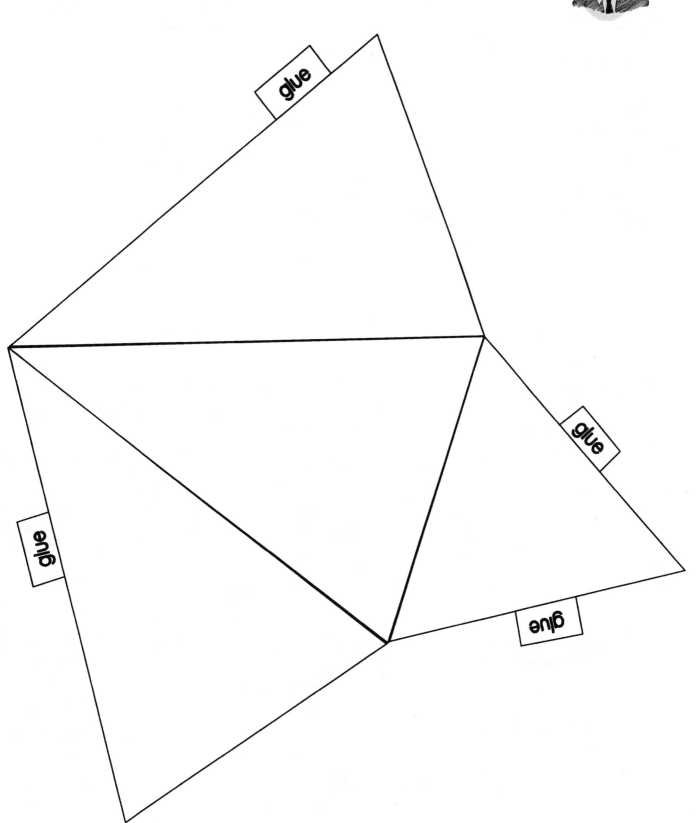

glue

glue

glue

glue

Dr. King's Birthday Dream Catcher

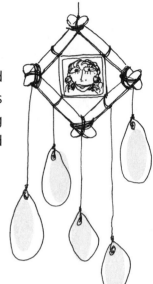

Native Americans used dream catchers to keep bad dreams away and to make sure that only good thoughts entered their minds at the moment between being awake and being asleep. Just as Dr. King talked of having a dream, this is a great project to inspire your students to remember and follow their own dreams. Just follow the directions and enjoy!

Materials

glue
crayons
thread
yarn
scissors
Popsicle sticks
colored yarn
paper
photo of each student

1. Glue the Popsicle sticks in the shape of a square. Let them dry completely.

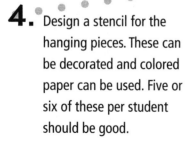

2. Use the colored yarn to decorate by wrapping it around the corners.

3. Use more yarn to make a square inside the square. Students' pictures will be glued on this inner square.

4. Design a stencil for the hanging pieces. These can be decorated and colored paper can be used. Five or six of these per student should be good.

5. Color and decorate the hanging pieces of the dream catcher. The pictures can be thematic or random.

6. Attach the hanging pieces to the Popsicle sticks using thread.

Dr. King's Birthday Teacher Resource Page

BULLETIN BOARD IDEA

- Title
- Colorful Border
- Student Question
- Rubric
- Children's Work
- Rubric Score/ Teacher Feedback
- Teacher Example
- State Standard

We All Have Dreams

What dream do you have that can change the world?

1.4 Students are able to recognize parts of their body.

Lesson Extensions

- This bulletin board can be a cross-circular extension of the MLK dream idea and science. Students trace their shadows on a piece of paper. Inside their shadows, they outline the brain and draw a picture of a dream they have had. Shadows can be shaded in as a silhouette.
- Extend this activity by having students trace their entire bodies on a sheet of paper and then adding parts of their bodies to their drawings. Internal body parts can include bones, muscles, and organs. Have fun with this one!
- After students have done the three positive things they can do to improve the world, choose some students to act out what they did and how people responded to their good deeds.

Word Bank

assassinated
race
equality
dream
leader
African American
judged
civil rights
character
demonstration

Children's Literature Ideas

Use for read-alouds, shared reading, silent reading, research, and so on.

Bray, R. (1996). *Martin Luther King.* William Morrow and Co. ISBN: 0688152198.

Farris, C. (2002). *My Brother Martin.* Simon and Schuster Children's. ISBN: 068943879.

McWhorter, D. (2004). *A Dream of Freedom.* Scholastic, Inc. ISBN: 0439576784.

Medearis, A. (2004). *Singing for Dr. King.* Teaching Resources. ISBN: 0439568552.

Rappaport, D. (2001). *Martin's Big Words.* Hyperion Books for Children. ISBN: 0786807148.

Chinese New Year

In China, Chinese New Year is a very important holiday. People take weeks to prepare for this important celebration. Depending on the lunar calendar in a given year, it is celebrated anywhere from late January to early February. The Chinese New Year always starts on a new moon and ends on the full moon 15 days later with the Lantern Festival—a time of family/community reunion. Each year is marked by an animal. Legend has it that Buddha, "the Awakened One" and founder of Buddhism, invited all the animals to meet him on New Year, but only 12 came. He named a year after each one, 12 in all. It is said that people born in a particular year would have some of the personality traits of that animal.

"*Gung Hay Fat Choy!*" is the Chinese greeting for the New Year. It is expressed in greetings, in children's picture books, and on packages and signs during this time of year. For centuries Chinese people have been welcoming in the New Year and chasing away the evil spirits by setting off firecrackers. Before fireworks, bamboo stalks were lit and the crackling flames were believed to frighten away evil spirits and bad luck. People wear red to symbolize fire, which also drives away bad luck, and children receive "lucky money" in special red envelopes.

The Lantern Festival marks the end of the Chinese New Year. A favorite part of this celebration to many is the Dragon Dance. Dragons can be as long as 100 feet. They are made out of silk, bamboo, and paper and are held up by people who weave it through the streets as they dance. This takes precision and coordination. The dragon's head is swayed, lifted, and swept around.

In cities where Chinese have settled, crowds gather in the streets of China-towns from New York to San Francisco for this huge celebration. Here in the United States the Dragon Dance is always held on a weekend with a traditional parade led by the huge cloth dragon that people support overhead as they dance through the streets. The dragon chases a red sun-ball or a white pearl-ball. The grasping of the ball means a full grip or control over luck and fortune in life. People playing drums and gongs follow the dragon. There are also traditional lion dancers with paper lion heads on sticks. As the parade moves along its way, store and business owners give the dancers money.

Finally, Chinese New Year is very important because every Chinese person celebrates his or her birthday on the New Year, regardless of the month in which he or she was actually born. Chinese people around the world celebrate.

Name: _____   Date: _____

Illustrate these four words:

lucky

drum

lion

dragon

Draw the dragon's body.

5 dragons were in the street.

6 lions joined them.

How many were there in all?

____ ◯ ____ = _____

Color and cut out the lion head. Mount on a pencil.

Name: _____   Date: _____

Illustrate these four words:

lucky

dragon

lantern

happiness

Chinese New Year is celebrated in

_____ .

Chinese New Year starts on

_____ .

What does every Chinese person celebrate on the New Year?

_____

Mary received $1.50, $3.75, and $2.65 from three store cashiers. What is the total amount of money she received?

Complete the dragon's body.

Color and cut out the lion head. Mount on a pencil.

Name: _____

Date: _____

Finish illustrating the Chinese New Year parade. Write about the celebration.

_____

_____

_____

Word Bank   China   drum   celebration   fireworks   happiness   dragon   lantern   lion   festival   lucky

Name: _____   Date: _____

Finish illustrating the Chinese New Year parade. Write about the celebration.

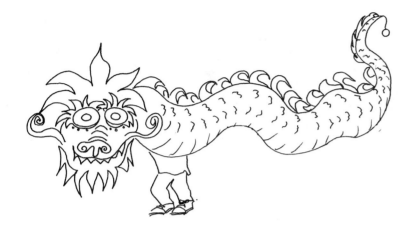

_____

_____

_____

_____

_____

_____

_____

_____

_____

_____

_____

_____

Word Bank   China   drum   celebration   fireworks   happiness   dragon   lantern   lion   festival   lucky

Build a Dragon

Chinese dragons are an important part of Chinese culture. They symbolize ultimate abundance, prosperity, and good fortune. Students can create their own dragons.

Materials

paper
scissors
glue
crayons
tissue paper
streamers or scrap paper

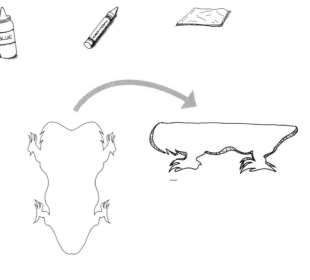

1. Color the dragon's head and body.
2. Cut out the body and fold it in half.
3. Decorate with a streamer tail, tissue paper, sequins, and so on.
4. Cut out the head and attach to the body.
5. Make a tail from streamers or scrap paper and attach.

20

Build a Dragon

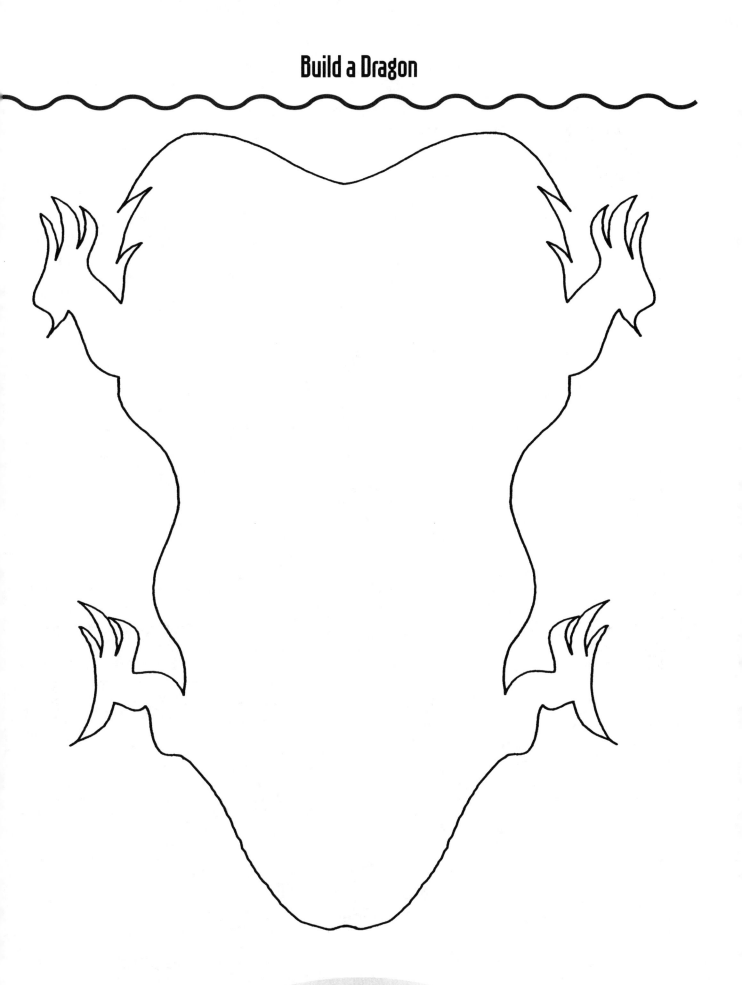

Build a Dragon Shadow Puppet

Shadow puppets were the first kind of puppet ever made. They originated in China. These puppets can cast detailed shadows onto a white sheet as they perform. Create your own shadow puppet.

Materials

chopsticks
paper
scissors
glue
crayons
brads or paper fasteners

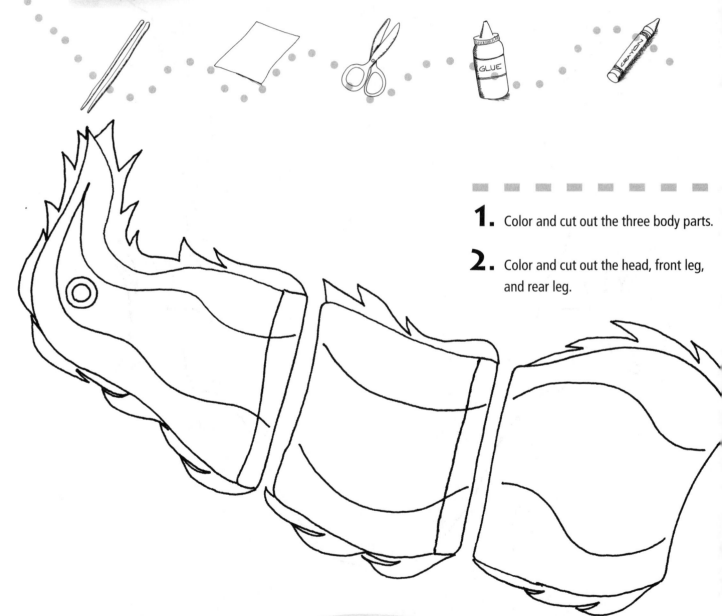

1. Color and cut out the three body parts.

2. Color and cut out the head, front leg, and rear leg.

Build a Dragon Shadow Puppet

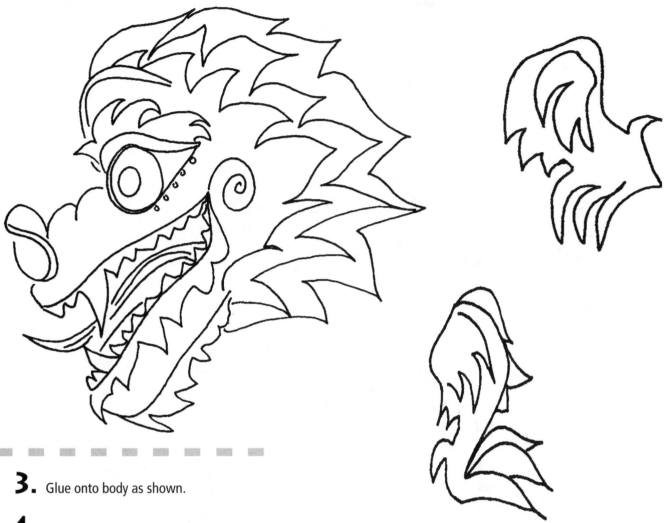

3. Glue onto body as shown.

4. Connect the body segments together with brads or paper fasteners.

5. Tape chopsticks to each body section. Use the chopsticks to make the finished puppet dance around your room.

Chinese Lanterns

Chinese lanterns help end the New Year with the Lantern Festival. These lanterns can be beautifully decorated and are carried in the festival under a full moon. Creating a Chinese lantern is fun and easy.

Materials

paper
scissors
glue

1. Fold paper in half.* Cut a series of straight lines from the fold to about an inch from the end. (Try variations and adjust to personal taste.)

2. Unfold the paper. Wrap around end-to-end. Sides will bow out slightly.

3. Glue together at the ends. Cut a separate strip of paper to make a handle. Glue both sides of the handle inside the top of the lantern.

* Try to draw a picture on the paper prior to cutting it to create a picture lantern. Pictures may include how they would celebrate the Chinese New Year or what they feel lucky for in their lives.

Write or illustrate four things you feel lucky for in your life.

Four things I am lucky for in life:

Chinese New Year Teacher Resource Page

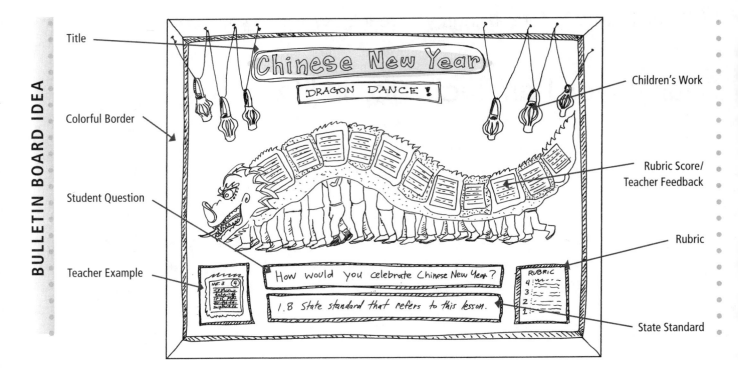

Title

Colorful Border

Student Question

Teacher Example

Children's Work

Rubric Score/
Teacher Feedback

Rubric

State Standard

Chinese New Year

DRAGON DANCE!

How would you celebrate Chinese New Year?

1.8 State standard that refers to this lesson.

RUBRIC
4
3
2
1

Lesson Extensions

- Have students write journal entries, mount them on colorful paper, and connect to create a dragon.
- Have a member of the local Chinese community—or someone who is very familiar with the holiday— speak to the class about the major customs associated with the Chinese New Year.
- Take a field trip to a Chinese restaurant or just order food from one for students to sample.

Word Bank

China
drums
celebration
fireworks
happiness
dragon
lantern
lion
festival
lucky

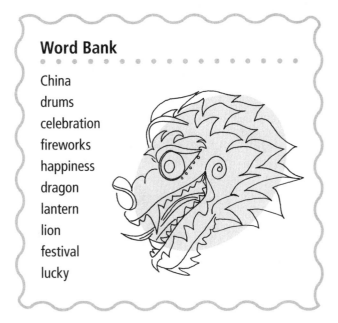

Children's Literature Ideas

Use for read-alouds, shared reading, silent reading, research, and so on.

Bouchard, D. (1999). *Dragon New Year.* Peachtree Publishing. ISBN:1561452106.

Chinn, K. (1997). *Sam and the Lucky Money.* Lee and Low Books, Inc. ISBN: 1880000539.

Hoyt-Goldsmith, D. (1999). *Celebrating the Chinese New Year.* Holiday House, Inc. ISBN: 0823415201.

Waters, K. (1990). *Lion Dancer.* Scholastic, Inc. ISBN: 0590430475.

Yep, K. (2004). *When the Circus Came to Town.* HarperCollins. ISBN: 0064409651.

Groundhog Day

Don't we all wish we could know when better weather is on the horizon? Wouldn't it be great to have a tool that could tell us when mild weather is in the forecast and that rain or snow is at its end? Well, we do have such a tool, but it is a bit different than a thermometer or weather forecaster!

On February 2 in the United States, everyone waits to see if the groundhog will see his shadow. At this time of the year—halfway between winter and spring—the groundhog starts to wake up from its winter hibernation. It is believed that if the groundhog sees its shadow, winter will continue for six more weeks. Shadows on a winter's day mean a very cold clear day, and so if the groundhog does not see its shadow, that is an indication spring is coming.

The origins of this tradition are most likely traced to Europe, where people long ago would watch other hibernating animals as an indication of winter's end. When German immigrants settled in Pennsylvania in the mid-1800s, local groundhogs became the hibernating creature of choice to watch. Through time, the tradition developed, and "Phil," the local groundhog of Punxsutawney, Pennsylvania, became the best-known celebrity groundhog, attracting media attention. In Canada, an albino groundhog

known as "Wiarton Willie" took on a similar popularity. He has been succeeded by his descendant, "Wee Willie."

Each year on February 2, watch for the news from Punxsutawney to see what Phil the Groundhog predicts as he emerges from his burrow. Maybe your local town has their own furry friend that does the same—such as "Brandon Bob" in Brandon (Manitoba), "Staten Island Chuck" in New York, "Balzac Billy" in Alberta, "Shubenacadie Sam" in Nova Scotia, and "Gary the Groundhog" in Kleinburg, Ontario, among many others. Have fun in your classroom with this wacky prognostication tradition!

Name: _____   Date: _____

| ground | hibernation | Phil | winter | burrow | sunshine |
| groundhog | February | shadow | emerge | hedgehog | |

Illustrate these four words:

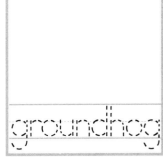
shadow

groundhog

winter

burrow

Estimate how many groundhogs can fit into the burrow.

Which one does *not* apply to a mammal? Cross it out.

milk   fur   egg   live birth

Measure my arms, legs, and height.

Finish drawing the groundhog.

Name: _____ Date: _____

Word Bank				
groundhog	February	shadow	emerge	hedgehog
hibernation	Phil	winter	burrow	sunshine

Illustrate these four words:

groundhog	*hibernate*	*burrow*	*emerge*

5 groundhogs all saw their shadows 5 minutes apart from each other. If the first groundhog saw his shadow at 8:05 A.M., when did the fifth groundhog see its shadow? What is the total time it took for all 5 to see their shadows?

Estimate how many groundhogs will fit in the burrow. Draw them.

Measure my arms and legs in inches and centimeters. What is their average length?

Finish drawing me and my shadow.

Name:

Date:

Finish the drawing. Write about what happens when the groundhog emerges from his burrow.

Word Bank groundhog hibernation February shadow winter emerge burrow hedgehog Phil sunshine

Name: _____   Date: _____

Write about what happened when the groundhog emerged from his burrow. Illustrate.

· ·

· ·

_____

_____

_____

_____

_____

_____

_____

_____

_____

_____

_____

_____

Word Bank   groundhog   hibernation   February   shadow   winter   emerge   burrow   hedgehog   Phil   sunshine

Pop-Up Groundhog

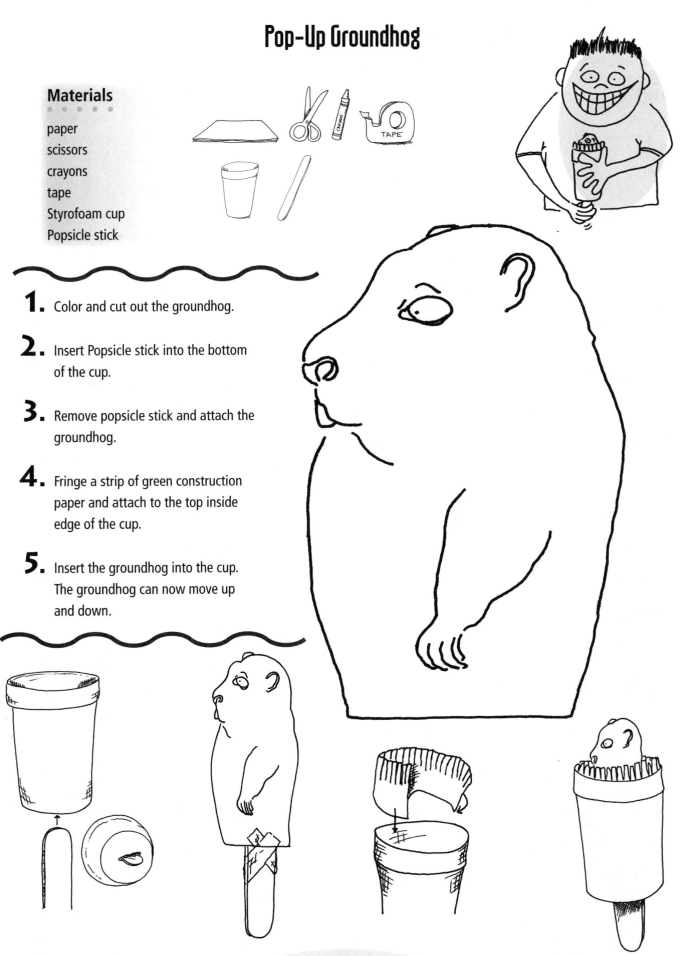

Materials

paper
scissors
crayons
tape
Styrofoam cup
Popsicle stick

1. Color and cut out the groundhog.

2. Insert Popsicle stick into the bottom of the cup.

3. Remove popsicle stick and attach the groundhog.

4. Fringe a strip of green construction paper and attach to the top inside edge of the cup.

5. Insert the groundhog into the cup. The groundhog can now move up and down.

Groundhogs in the Grass

Materials

paper
scissors
crayons
tape

1. Color and cut out groundhogs.

2. Fold groundhogs in half to stand.

3. Color, cut out, and tape grass ring.

4. Create a story problem of groundhogs in the grass and groundhogs out of the grass. Then determine sums, differences, fractions, or percents.

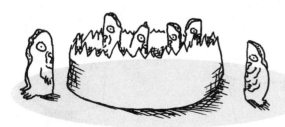

Groundhog Day Teacher Resource Page

Title
Children's Work
Student Question
Teacher Example

Colorful Border
Rubric Score/Teacher Feedback
Rubric
State Standard

How many different ways can you make 20.

2.4 State standard that refers to this lesson.

Lesson Extensions

- Use the Groundhogs in the Grass activity to create an interactive math bulletin board.
- Tie this holiday into a lesson on mammals.
- Research groundhogs on the Internet. Write groundhog reports.
- Watch a video on groundhogs or mammals in general.

Word Bank

groundhog
hibernation
February
shadow
winter
emerge
burrow
hedgehog
Phil
sunshine

Children's Literature Ideas

Use for read-alouds, shared reading, silent reading, research, and so on.

Freeman, D. (2003). *Gregory's Shadow*. Penguin. ISBN: 0142301965.

Korman, S. (1998). *Wakeup Groundhog!* Random House. ISBN: 0307988481.

McMullan, K. (2001). *Fluffy Meets the Groundhog*. Scholastic, Inc. ISBN: 0439206723.

McNamara, M. (2005). *Groundhog Day*. Simon and Schuster. ISBN: 1416905073.

Pickford, S. (1993). *It's Up to You, Griffin!* Cornell Maritime Press. ISBN: 0870334468.

Valentine's Day

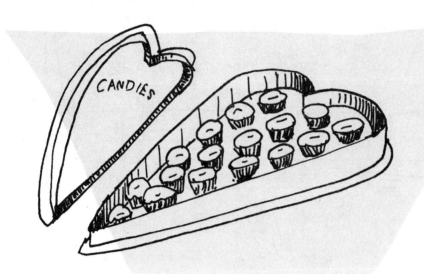

What do you do on a daily basis to celebrate the love you have for family and friends? Do you say, "I love you"? Do you do small favors for those in need? You can always count on Valentine's Day, February 14, as a day to show our love and appreciation. Today we celebrate Valentine's Day by sending greeting cards, candy, flowers, or gifts to loved ones and friends, while classrooms are often decorated with pink and red paper hearts.

The idea of a holiday to celebrate romance and love can be traced back to Roman times, when a festival celebrating the Roman deity Lupercalia was held. There are several stories of how the festival was celebrated. In one version, young men wearing goat skins ran through the city lightly striking women with strips of goat skin to ensure fertility. In another version, the names of all the young women were placed in a box and then drawn by each young man, and those couples would be paired during the festival. As early as A.D. 496, Christians were celebrating the feast of St. Valentine, although its meaning as a day to exchange devotions of romantic love really didn't take hold until the 19th century.

Some believe that sending poetic love letters started when Charles, the Duke of Orleans, was captured during the Battle of Agincourt and sent love letters of rhyming

poetry to his wife from his cell in the Tower of London. Whatever the actual origins, today you can use the holiday as a jumping-off point for your own unique lesson on friendship and love.

A traditional figure on many Valentine's Day cards is Cupid, the god of love in Roman mythology. His equivalent in Greek mythology is Eros, and another Latin name is Amor, which means "love." In any incarnation, he carries a bow and arrows, which dispense love and romance to the recipient.

Since Valentine's Day is from the heart, it is important to remember that a simple hug or hand-drawn card is just as welcome as gifts and flowers.

Name: **Date:**

Illustrate these four words:

candy   card   heart   love

Which heart has equal parts? Circle it.

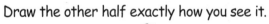

Make another shape and divide it into equal parts.

Draw three things that remind you of Valentine's Day (e.g., gift, flowers, card, or candy).

Draw the other half exactly how you see it.

On the back of this paper, write a card for someone special. Use the following guide:

DATE:
TO:
MESSAGE:

LOVE,

Name: _____   Date: _____

Illustrate these four words:

family

heart

chocolate

card

Senai had 344 candy hearts. If she gave 4 of her friends equal amounts, how many candies would each friend get? Show your work.

Research and label the parts of the heart.

_____   _____

_____   _____

List all the people you care about and their relationship to you.

Name · · · · · · · · · · · · **Relationship** · · · · · · · · ·

_____   _____

_____   _____

_____   _____

_____   _____

_____   _____

Design the cover of your own Valentine's Day card.

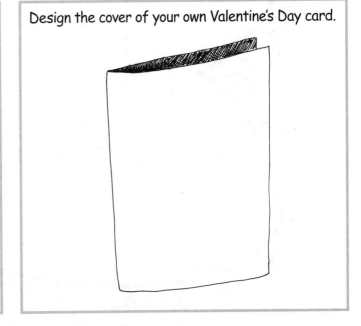

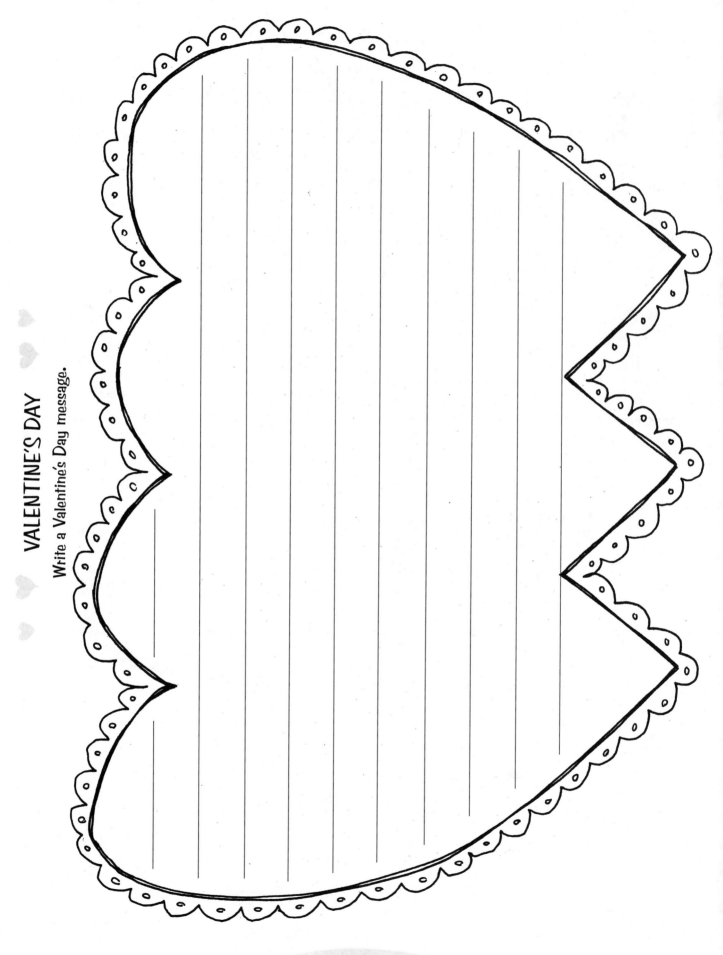

VALENTINE'S DAY

Write a Valentine's Day message.

Name: _____

Date: _____

Write about all the things that you love, that you care about, and that mean a lot to you! Illustrate when finished.

_____

_____

_____

_____

_____

_____

_____

_____

_____

_____

_____

Castle of Rhyming Words

Design your own castle and practice reading rhyming words. Once the castle is made, students can cut out the hearts with words on them. The words that rhyme can be put on the outside of the castle, fitting into the bricks, and the words that don't rhyme can be dropped into the castle "jail." Try using the blank heart to make other words for a different game.

1. Cut out the castle.

2. Cut out the window on the dotted line.

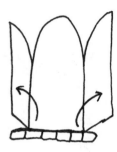

3. Fold open the doors of the windows.

4. Cut the dotted lines above the bricks on the castle.

5. Glue the castle together after all the dotted lines have been cut.

6. Glue the king into the castle window as shown.

7. Place the hearts that have rhyming words in the slits on the castle bricks.

8. Put the words that don't rhyme inside the castle "jail."

9. You have your finished castle!

42

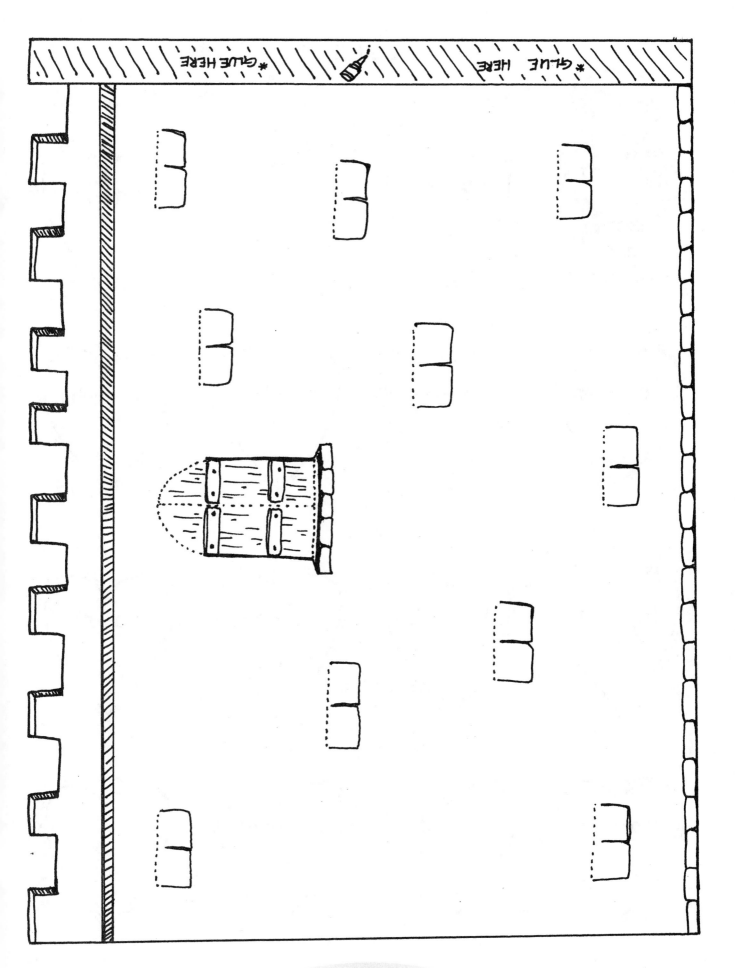

Castle of Rhyming Words

fun—sun

rat—mat

hit—fit

pop—hop

run—bat

red—bed

ship—whip

fan—not

stop—drop

fan—tan

top—sit

clap—trap

brat—plot

get—net

? ?

Valentine's Day Hearts Game

In this matching game, paper hearts are cut in half after writing one word on each side of the heart. Use the hearts on the next page and make several copies for each student. Each student will also make an envelope to hold his or her game pieces.

The words should be antonyms or synonyms (or something else that can match—teacher's choice). The game is won after a student is able to match all hearts after they have been mixed up.

1. Cut out hearts.

2. Write words on each side of the heart.

3. Cut hearts in half.

4. Cut out envelope.

5. Fold envelope and glue flaps.

6. Mix up all the pieces of paper hearts and put them inside the envelope.

7. Decorate the envelope.

8. Match the words to make a heart.

9. Finish matching all of the words to complete the game!

Valentine's Day Hearts Game

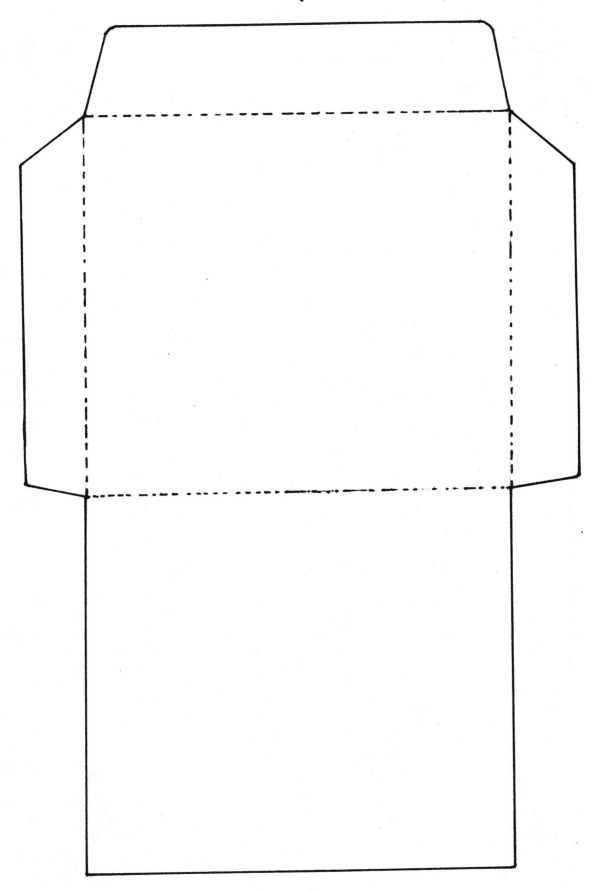

47

© The McGraw-Hill Companies, Inc.

Name: _____

Date: _____

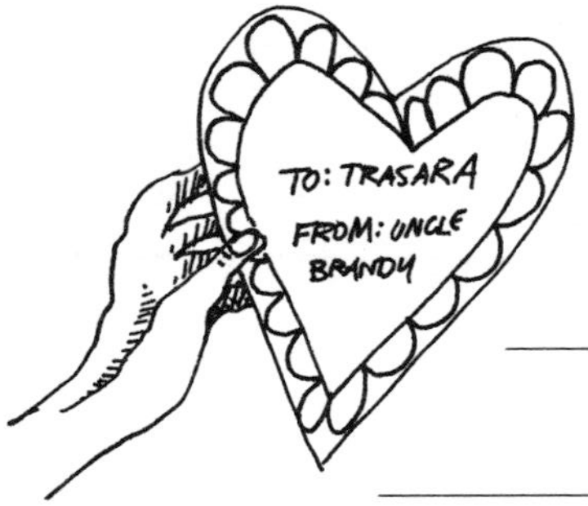

Class List of Names for Valentine's Day Cards

TO: MRS. KWONG
FROM: RIZZEL
HAPPY VALENTINES DAY
LOVE

BE MY VALENTINE

TO: TRASARA
FROM: UNCLE
BRANDY

BE MINE?

Valentine's Day Teacher Resource Page

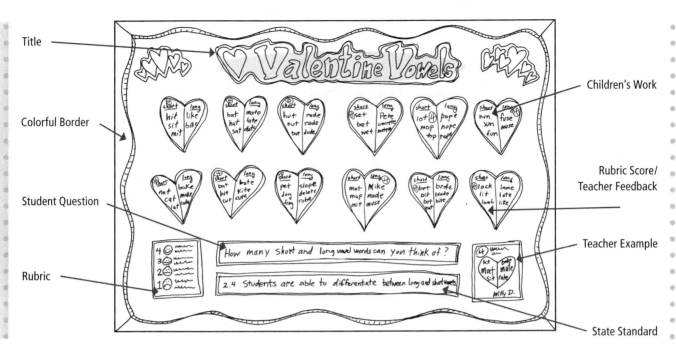

Labels on the bulletin board diagram:
- Title
- Colorful Border
- Student Question
- Rubric
- Children's Work
- Rubric Score/Teacher Feedback
- Teacher Example
- State Standard

Bulletin board title: **Valentine Vowels**

Student Question: How many short and long vowel words can you think of?

State Standard: 2.4 Students are able to differentiate between long and short vowels

Lesson Extensions

- Use hearts to make a bulletin board display of word family lists, thematic lists, fact families, and so on.
- Hearts can be decorated with a specialty paper or some type of lace.
- Create valentines for family members and friends.
- Large hearts can include a poem or a story on one side and an illustration on the other side.

Word Bank

February
candy
card
heart
friendship
love
family
caring
kinship
chocolate

Children's Literature Ideas

Use for read-alouds, shared reading, silent reading, research, and so on.

Fradin, D. (1990). *Valentine's Day.* Enslow Publishers, Inc. ISBN: 084902377.

Landau, E. (2002). *Valentine's Day: Candy, Love, and Hearts.* Enslow Publishers, Inc. ISBN: 0766017796.

Marney, D. (2001). *How to Drive Your Family Crazy . . . on Valentine's Day.* Apple Publishing. ISBN: 0439158494.

Rau, D. (2001). *Valentine's Day.* Sagebrush Education Resources. ISBN: 0613516885.

Presidents' Day

residents' Day is celebrated in the United States on the third Monday of February. This date, designated a federal holiday by Congress, was originally intended to honor the birthday of George Washington, our nation's first President. Through time, the day has come to be a day to honor all former U.S. Presidents but especially Washington and Abraham Lincoln, whose birthday is also in February. Presidents' Day is a day to celebrate the accomplishments and contributions of these very special American leaders.

George Washington served as a general in the army during the Revolutionary War against Britain and was then elected the first U.S. President under America's newly adopted Constitution. Because of his importance in our nation's history, George Washington's birthday was designated a national holiday as far back in U.S. history as 1885.

Abraham Lincoln, born on February 12, 1809, was our nation's 13th President. As a boy Abraham loved to read. He was known as "Honest Abe" because at one point in his young life he walked through the snow to return money that was given to him by mistake. As U.S. President, Lincoln freed the slaves and abolished slavery forever.

It is because of their great contributions to our nation that we remember these two Presidents, as well as all our Presidents and their contributions, on Presidents' Day.

Name: _____   Date: _____

Illustrate these four words:

Washington	Lincoln	penny	quarter

How much money is there in all?

_____ ¢

Circle which device Washington or Lincoln would use to write.

Draw or cut out and paste a picture of the correct U.S. President on each bill. Color the money.

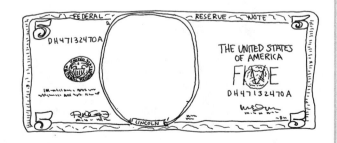

Name: _____   Date: _____

Word Bank				
President	Lincoln	celebrate	national	quarter
Washington	birthday	honor	penny	dollar

Illustrate these four words:

Washington   _Lincoln_   _penny_   _quarter_

Linda has the money shown below. She wants to buy a dog bed for $24.95. How much more money does she need?

Finish the drawing of General Washington.

Presidential Facts

_____ became our nation's first President in _____.

_____ _____ freed the slaves and was

our _____ President. Presidents' Day is celebrated

on _____.

Draw pictures of George Washington and Abraham Lincoln on the correct money.

 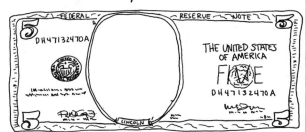

Name: _____

Date: _____

Finish illustrating the pictures. *Write about why we remember George Washington and Abraham Lincoln.*

_____

_____

_____

_____

Word Bank   President   Washington   Lincoln   birthday   celebrate   honor   national   penny   quarter   dollar

Name: ______________________ Date: ______________

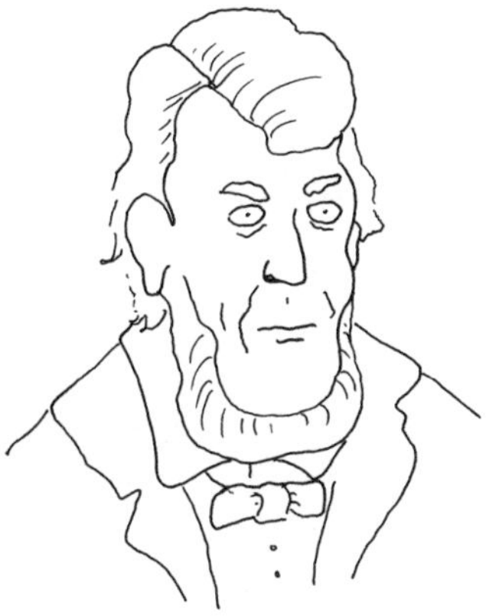

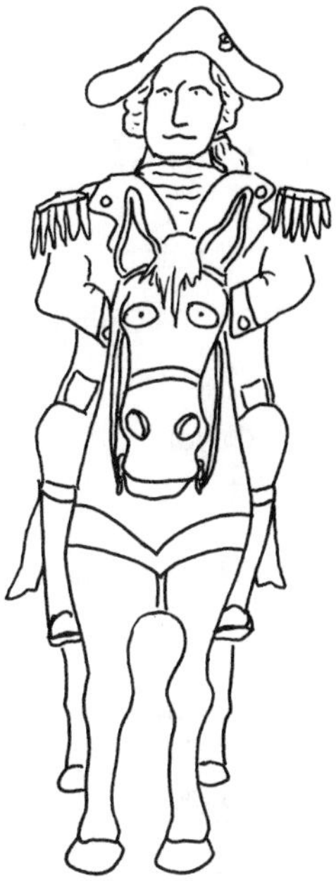

Finish illustrating the pictures. Write about why we remember George Washington and Abraham Lincoln.

Word Bank President Washington Lincoln birthday celebrate honor national penny quarter dollar

Presidential Silhouettes

Create a stencil from the silhouette. Trace over paper and cut out. Glue onto construction paper.

Materials

silhouette
construction paper
scissors
crayons
glue

1.

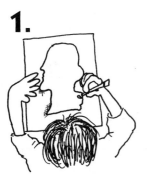

2.

3.

Presidential Silhouettes

Other Ideas

Create silhouette art.

Write a story.

Illustrate an event.

Draw in the face.

Create a giant coin.

Presidents' Day Teacher Resource Page

Title

Colorful Border

Student Question

Teacher Example

Children's Work

Rubric Score/ Teacher Feedback

Rubric

State Standard

Lesson Extensions

- Create a coin bulletin board. Students can count coins and list the Presidents on their coins for a designated amount of money.
- Write a letter to the current President describing what you think he or she is doing well or what he or she could do better.
- Write a letter to George Washington or Abraham Lincoln telling him why you respect his efforts as President.

Word Bank

President
Washington
Lincoln
birthday
celebrate
honor
national
penny
quarter
dollar

Children's Literature Ideas

Use for read-alouds, shared reading, silent reading, research, and so on.

Davis, K. (2001). *Don't Know Much About the Presidents.* HarperCollins. ISBN: 0060286156.

Deutsch, S. & Cohon, R. (2005). *Lincoln's Legacy.* Aladdin. ISBN: 068980238.

Ditchfield, C. (2003). *Presidents' Day.* Children's Press. ISBN: 051622784X.

Dodson, M. (2004). *Presidents' Day.* Enslow Publishers, Inc. ISBN: 076602234X.

MacMillan, D. (1997). *Presidents' Day.* Enslow Publishers, Inc. ISBN: 0894908200.

St. Patrick's Day

Don't forget to wear green today or you'll get pinched! Everyone is Irish on St. Patrick's Day, celebrated each year on March 17, the anniversary of the death of St. Patrick, patron saint of Ireland. On this holiday everyone traditionally wears green, which is the color of a shamrock, a three-leaf clover that is the national symbol of Ireland. Those not "wearin' of the green" are said to get pinched.

Little is known for certain about the man behind the legends, but it is believed that St. Patrick's name at birth was Maewyn Succat and that he was born at the end of the fourth century in Roman Britain, in an area that is today part of Wales. As

the legend goes, when he was 16 years old he was kidnapped by a band of Irish pirates and sold into slavery in Ireland, where he worked as a shepherd for 6 years. During his enslavement, he turned to God for comfort. After his escape, he returned to his family, took the name Patrick, and began his studies for the priesthood.

It took many years to become a priest, and when he was finally ordained, he felt his calling was to return to Ireland and convert the heathen to Christianity. Through the many years that he traveled the Irish countryside, he converted an untold number of people, established monasteries, ordained new

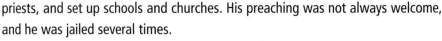

priests, and set up schools and churches. His preaching was not always welcome, and he was jailed several times.

There were dozens of legends about St. Patrick's life and teachings. Some say he raised the dead. A popular legend is that he drove the snakes out of Ireland after a sermon, even though Ireland never had native snakes. One of the most enduring legends, and the one most likely true, involved his use of the shamrock, a native plant in Ireland, to explain the concept of the Holy Trinity in Christianity. The plant has three leaves, and St. Patrick used the three leaves of one plant to represent idea of the Father, Son, and Holy Ghost still only being one God. The shamrock is today the national flower of Ireland, and it is commonly worn on lapels for good luck.

Patrick eventually grew old and retired to County Down, where he died on March 17, 461. The day he died is now commemorated as St. Patrick's Day.

The first major St. Patrick's Day celebration in the United States was in Boston, Massachusetts, in 1737. Today, St. Patrick's Day is celebrated each year across the United States on March 17. Many cities celebrate by holding St. Patrick's Day parades. Everything seems to turn green in celebration of this very green holiday. Cookies, baked goods, and even beverages are colored green in the spirit of the day. The city of Chicago, with its large Irish population, even dyes the Chicago River green as part of the fun. Everywhere people celebrate with traditional foods such as Irish stew, corn beef and cabbage with rye bread, and potatoes and onions.

Shamrocks decorate classrooms along with leprechauns, Irish fairies that are said to have a hidden pot of gold. As the story goes, if you can catch a leprechaun you may be able to get him to tell you where his pot of gold is hidden!

Name: _____   Date: _____

Word Bank					
	green	shamrock	Irish	leprechaun	March
	St. Patrick	clover	parade	gold	pinch

Illustrate these four words:

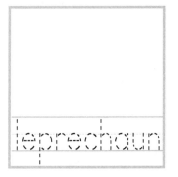

leprechaun

shamrock

green

gold

Illustrate and write the number sentence.

7 gold coins are in the pot.
8 more are added to the pot.

How many gold coins are
in the pot in all?

____ ◯ ____ = ____

Label the parts of a clover/shamrock.

leaf

stem

root

Finish drawing the leprechaun.

Color all the matching clovers the same color.

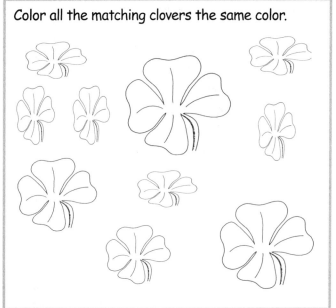

Name: _____   Date: _____

| green | shamrock | Irish | leprechaun | March |
| St. Patrick | clover | parade | gold | pinch |

Illustrate these four words:

leprechaun

shamrock

parade

gold

There are 16 four-leaf clovers and 21 clovers. How many leaves are there in all?

Label the parts of a clover.

_____

_____

_____

Finish drawing the leprechaun.

St. Patrick's Day Facts

St. Patrick's Day is celebrated _____.

St. Patrick's name was _____.

Legend claims he chased _____

out of Ireland.

The first St. Patrick's Day was celebrated in

_____.

Name: _____ Date: _____

Finish illustrating the picture. Write about a leprechaun adventure.

_____

_____

_____

Word Bank   green   St. Patrick   shamrock   clover   Irish   parade   leprechaun   gold   March   pinch

Name: Date:

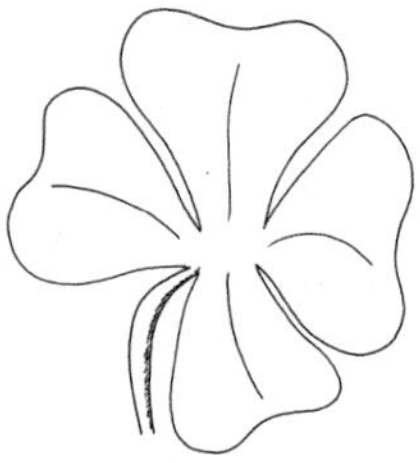

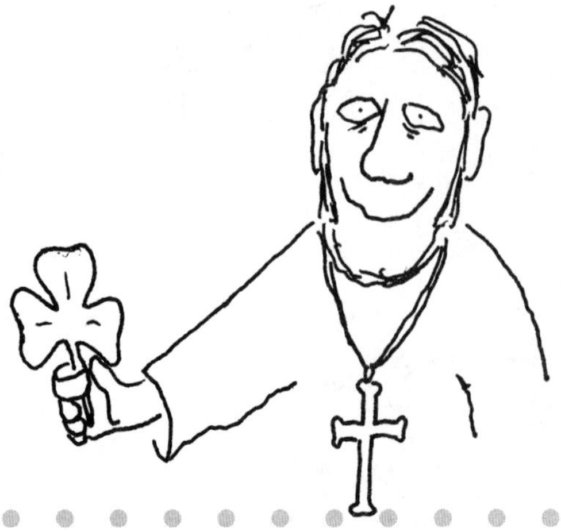

Finish illustrating the picture. Write about the history of St. Patrick's Day and how we celebrate this holiday today.

Word Bank green St. Patrick shamrock clover Irish parade leprechaun gold March pinch

Build a Leprechaun

Materials

paper
scissors
brads
crayons

Build a Leprechaun

1. Color the leprechaun and his arms and legs.

2. Cut out the parts.

3. Assemble with brads.

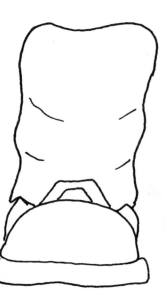

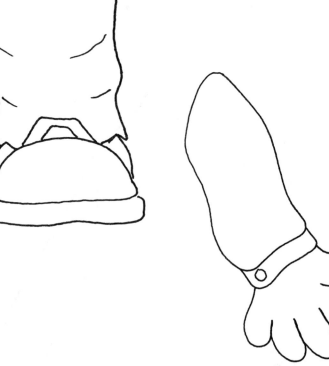

Pot of Gold

There are many different uses for this project. Try writing vocabulary, spelling words, math facts, or matching words (e.g., rhyming, antonyms, or synonyms) on the coins. Color and cut out. Place on pot and use as a practice and review.

St. Patrick's Day Teacher Resource Page

BULLETIN BOARD IDEA

Title

Colorful Border

Student Question

Teacher Example

Children's Work

Rubric Score/
Teacher Feedback

Rubric

State Standard

(Bulletin board labels) Character Clover — How do you describe your character from the fable? — 7.8 State standard that refers to this activity. — RUBRIC 4 3 2 1

Lesson Extensions

- Have students create a Character Clover bulletin board describing characters from a fable or a story. Each leaf would describe a characteristic of the character.
- Have a class party and bring in traditional Irish foods such as corn beef and cabbage stew.
- Have students write a letter to their parent or guardian stating all the things they have been lucky for in life.

Word Bank

green
St. Patrick
shamrock
clover
Irish
parade
leprechaun
gold
March
pinch

Children's Literature Ideas

Use for read-alouds, shared reading, silent reading, research, and so on.

Calamary, B. & Redeker, K. (2002). *Green with Envy.* Simon Spotlight Publishing. ISBN: 0689845839.

Freeman, D. (1992). *St. Patrick's Day.* Enslow Publishers, Inc. ISBN: 0894903837.

Landau, E. (2002). *St. Patrick's Day.* Enslow Publishers, Inc. ISBN: 076601777X.

Nolan, J. (2002). *St. Patrick's Day Shillelagh.* Albert Whitman Publishers. ISBN: 0807573442.

Rue, N. (2005). *Sophie's Irish Showdown.* Zonderkidz Publishing. ISBN: 0310707595.

Easter

Easter is not only about dyed eggs, hollow chocolate bunnies, marshmallow chicks, baskets, egg hunts, and the like. Easter has very special religious significance for many, and most of the holiday's contemporary traditions are derived from its history.

For Christians, Easter celebrates the resurrection of Jesus Christ, the Son of God. But Easter also has pagan elements in today's celebrations that have nothing to do with Christianity. These pagan elements take Easter back to its roots, where the Scandinavian goddess of spring, "Eastre," and the Teutonic goddess of fertility, "Ostern," were celebrated. The celebration represented the triumph over death and coincided with the timing of Easter. These goddesses of spring and fertility were celebrated on the vernal equinox, the first day of spring. The word "Easter" is believed to be derived from their names.

The vernal equinox falls on March 21, but Easter always falls on the Sunday following the full moon around this time. So Easter can happen anywhere from March 22 to as late as April 25.

One of the modern traditions associated with this pagan celebration of spring is the Easter bunny. Rabbits have been a symbol of fertility. The modern Easter bunny is believed to have originated in Germany, where an "Easter hare" was said to have laid eggs for children to find.

This tradition was brought to the United States by German immigrants. They even baked cakes in the shape of rabbits—which could be how the tradition of today's chocolate bunnies eventually began.

Another tradition associated with this pagan spring celebration of long ago is the Easter egg itself. The eggs traditionally colored with bright colors represented the sunlight of spring and symbolized new life and fertility. Throughout history there were other influences on the modern-day Easter egg. Eggs were forbidden in Medieval Europe during Lent, so they were usually preserved by boiling them. When Easter arrived they were a major part of the meal and even a prize for servant children. Orthodox Christians painted eggs red for the blood of Christ. Other countries painted religious depictions of Easter on eggs. In some Eastern European countries, the eggs were elaborately painted and decorated.

Today Easter has become a time of Easter bunnies and Easter egg hunts. Children eagerly wait for the Easter bunny to fill their baskets with jelly beans, chocolate bunnies, brightly colored plastic eggs filled with candy, and marshmallow chicks. These are all popular modern-day Easter traditions. However for those of the Christian faith, Easter time is a very important part of the year. It starts with the 46-day period of Lent—a time of self-reflection and forgiveness—that leads up to Easter. Lent begins with Ash Wednesday, when an ash cross is smudged on one's forehead as he or she asks for forgiveness. The last week of Lent starts with Palm Sunday, symbolic of when Jesus rode into Jerusalem and palms were laid at his feet. Holy Thursday of that week represents the Last Supper, the night before Jesus was crucified. Friday, or Good Friday, represents the day of the crucifixion. Three days later is Easter Sunday, which represents the day Jesus is said to have risen from the dead.

Today, children wake up early on Easter and search for their Easter baskets, which they either fill (or which have already been filled) with treats, small gifts, and dyed eggs. While this is fun, one must remember the history of Easter be it through its Christian or its pagan roots. Visiting the Easter bunny, receiving an Easter basket, and partaking in Easter egg hunts are the commercial aspects of today's Easter celebrations, but for many it is a religious holiday that is the cornerstone of their faith.

Name: _____   Date: _____

Illustrate these four words:

eggs

basket

bunny

family

Trasara collects 8 red eggs, 5 blue eggs, and 13 yellow eggs. How many eggs does she have altogether?

Which picture below does not belong with Easter? Cross it out.

Which one of the items below is made with eggs? Circle it. Below the pictures list some other items that are made with eggs.

_____

_____

_____

Finish drawing and color the other half of the Easter egg.

Word Bank

eggs	hunt	celebration	bunny	spring
basket	decorations	feast	family	dye

Illustrate these four words:

feast   _celebration_   _spring_   _decorations_

Mr. Stockstill's class went on an Easter egg hunt. There are 20 students in his class. 8 students found 8 red eggs each, 10 students found 5 blue eggs each, and 2 students found 9 yellow eggs each. How many eggs did the class find in all?

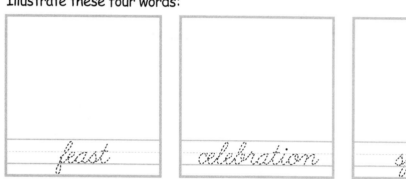

Research and label the parts of the egg.

Finish drawing the other half of the rabbit and color.

Design your own Easter basket.

Name: _____

Date: _____

Illustrate what you write about in your journal. Use the vocabulary words to write about how you celebrate Easter.

_____

_____

_____

_____

Word Bank eggs   basket   hunt   decorations   celebration   feast   bunny   family   spring   dye

Name: _____

Easter Egg Journal: Write about how you celebrate Easter.

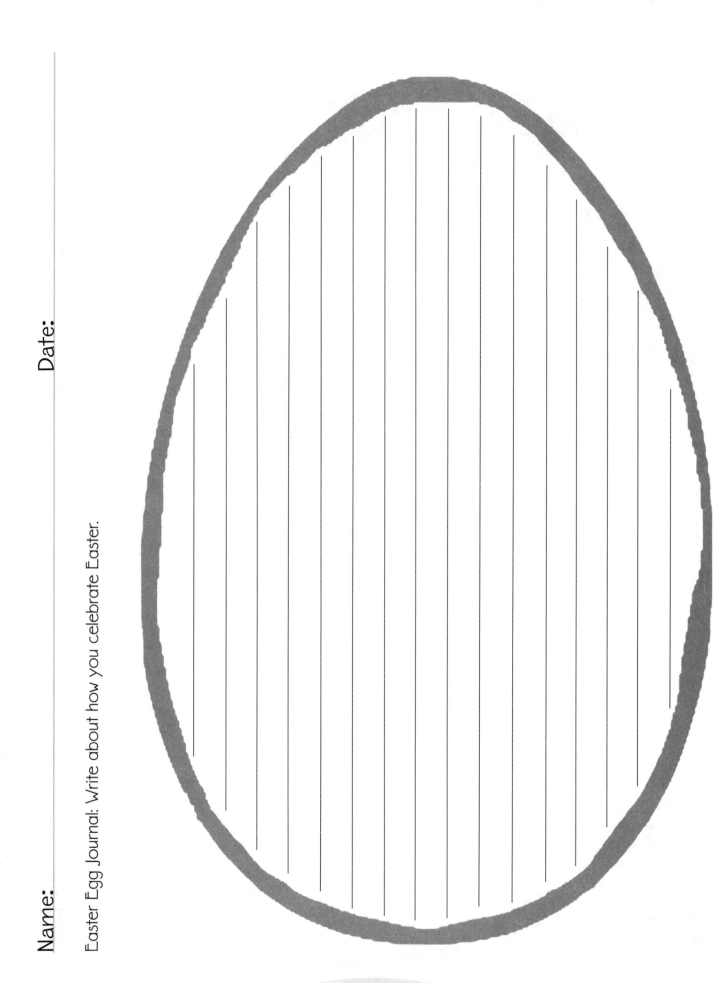

Easter Bunny Bag

An Easter Bunny Bag can be a great way to culminate your activities around Easter. Students can add cards, candy, and even Easter eggs that they contribute to the celebration.

Materials

small brown paper bags
crayons
glue
scissors
white pipe cleaners (optional)
cotton balls (optional)

1. Give students both pages. Have them color them and cut them out.

2. Glue all the parts of the bunny to the brown bag. (Optional: Use white pipe cleaners for the bunny's whiskers and a cotton ball for the tail!)

3. Put bags on desks and fill with candy, cards, and eggs!

Easter Bunny Bag

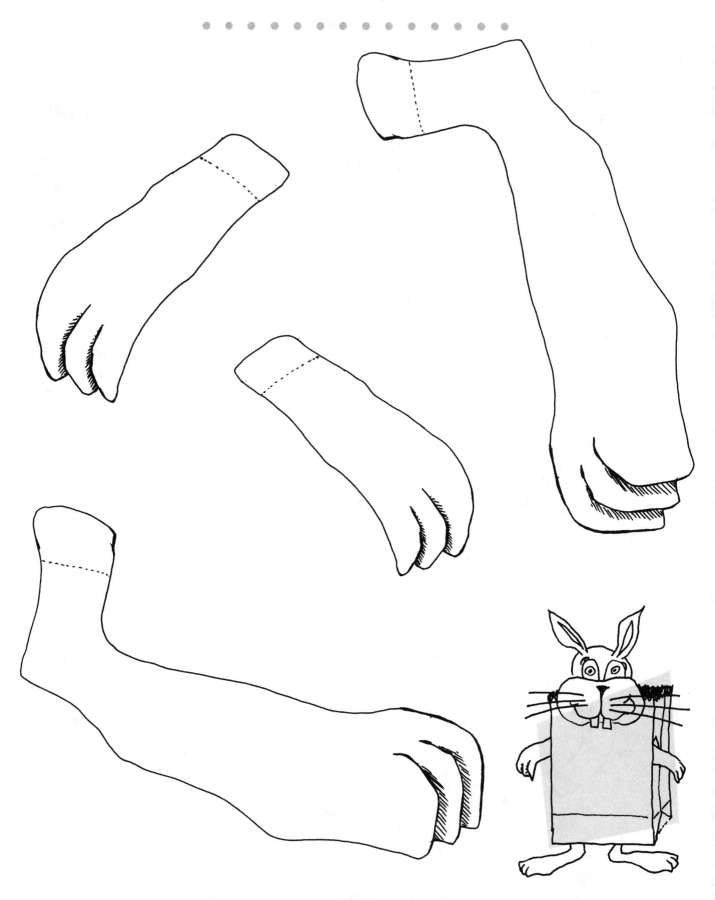

Easter Teacher Resource Page

Title — Eggcellent Recipe

Children's Work

Colorful Border

Rubric Score/
Teacher Feedback

Student Question

How many eggs does your recipe require?

Rubric

Teacher Example — Mr. Wesley

7.7 State Standard that refers to this activity

State Standard

Lesson Extensions

- Write recipes that use eggs as an ingredient. Recipes can come from home, out of a book, or off the Internet.
- Create living Easter baskets using plastic one-pint strawberry baskets lined with cellophane. Fill with vermiculite soil and plant wheat berries. Baskets will grow real grass and can be filled with eggs and wrapped candies.
- Have an Easter egg hunt.
- Use plastic eggs and fill with matching words. Have each student read his or her word and find the other student with the word that matches. (You can use antonyms, synonyms, vowel patterns, and so on.)

Word Bank

eggs
basket
hunt
decorations
celebration
feast
bunny
family
spring
dye

Children's Literature Ideas

Use for read-alouds, shared reading, silent reading, research, and so on.

Blizin-Gillais, J. (2005). *My Easter.* Raintree Publishers. ISBN: 1410907805.

Carlson, M. (2004). *The Easterville Miracle.* B&H Publishing. ISBN: 0805426809.

Korman, J. (2004). *The Grumpy Easter Bunny.* Scholastic, Inc. ISBN: 0439635950.

Maier, P. (2000). *Very First Easter.* Concordia Publishing. ISBN: 0570070538.

Sanders, N. (2003). *Easter.* Children's Press. ISBN: 0516277774.

April Fools' Day

Who doesn't enjoy playing tricks on people? Just be sure to keep the tricks safe and jovial, not inappropriate or unsafe!

How the tradition of April Fools' Day started is not exactly clear. It was initially called "All Fools' Day" and seems to have been a folk celebration that began in Europe during the late Middle Ages. "All Fools' Day" was traditionally devoted to foolery.

One possible explanation for how April Fools' Day started goes back to 16th-century France. During that time New Year was actually observed on the first day of April, not January 1 as it is today. But in 1582 Pope Gregory changed the calendar from the Julian calendar to the Gregorian calendar. The first day of this new calendar was January 1, which most of the world uses today. During the switch to the new calendar, some people didn't hear of the change, didn't believe there was a change, or refused to accept the change. These people continued to celebrate New Year's Day on April 1, instead of January 1. As a result, they were often teased or tricked and called "April fools." One type of trick was sending non-believers on a "fool's errand" in search of something that did not exist. Another trick was to try to make them believe something that was not true. Through time this joking practice on April 1 spread throughout Europe.

Today the tradition continues. In the United States, people still play small tricks on one another. Once the trick is discovered, the prankster calls out "April fools!" and the victim knows they have been had. These are meant to be harmless practical jokes, all in good fun. This is important. It's no longer fun if the joke or prank turns dangerous or hurtful. So on April Fools' Day be prepared for fun!

Name: _____   Date: _____

Illustrate these four words:

prank

laughter

silly

victim

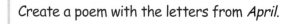

On April Fools' Day, Ben used his hand buzzer prank on 5 boys and 8 girls. How many students did he pull his prank on in all? How many more girls than boys did he pull his prank on?

Create a poem with the letters from *April*.

A

P

R

I

L

The class scared Miguel with a rubber spider. It looked real!

It had _____ legs.

It had _____ body parts.

It had _____ antennae.

Draw what April Fools' Day joke made Maria laugh.

Name: _____   Date: _____

| joke | laughter | funny | fool | victim |
| prank | harmless | humorous | errand | silly |

Illustrate these four words:

humorous	*joke*	*prank*	*victim*

There are 20 students in the class, and 10 pranks were played. Thirty percent of the students had a prank played on them. How many students had pranks played on them? What percent and number of students did not have pranks played on them?

Write your own knock-knock joke.

Knock, knock!

Who's there?

_____ .

_____ who?

_____ !

Students used rubber spiders and rubber insects to play pranks on other students for April Fools' Day. Draw and label an insect and a spider. Include the correct number of body parts, legs, and antennae.

_____ Spider   _____ Insect

Draw a face reacting to a prank.

Name: _____

Date: _____

Write about an April Fools' Day joke that you would play on a friend. Illustrate it.

_____

_____

_____

Word Bank   joke   prank   laughter   harmless   funny   humorous   fool   errand   victim   silly

Who would you like to play an April Fools' Day joke on? Why would you like to do this, and what would the joke be? Write and illustrate the scenario.

_____

_____

_____

_____

_____

_____

_____

_____

_____

_____

_____

_____

Word Bank   joke   prank   laughter   harmless   funny   humorous   fool   errand   victim   silly

Trick Spider

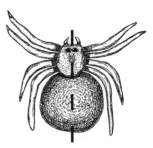

Create a trick spider to trick your friends.

Materials

paper
scissors
string
crayons

1. Color the spider.
2. Cut out spider and fold down the middle to stand your spider like a tent.

3. Fold legs three times to stand the spider up off the floor.

4. Attach a string, thread, or piece of fishing line to the front of your spider.

5. Place your spider on the floor and slowly pull it along.

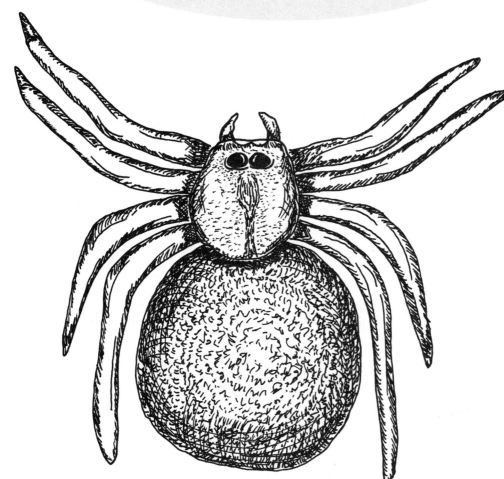

April Fools' Day Teacher Resource Page

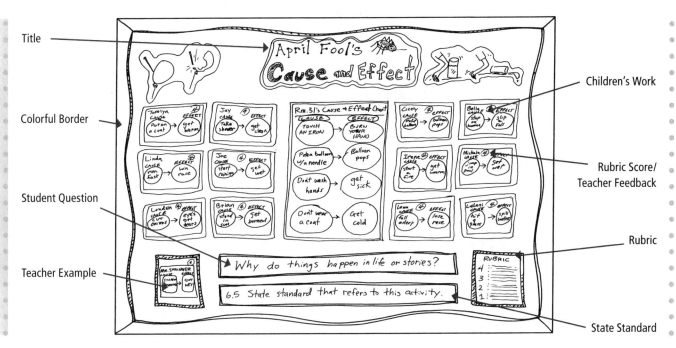

Title

Colorful Border

Student Question

Teacher Example

Children's Work

Rubric Score/Teacher Feedback

Rubric

State Standard

April Fool's Cause and Effect

Why do things happen in life or stories?

6.5 State standard that refers to this activity.

Lesson Extensions

- Create a Cause and Effect bulletin board. Use pranks as Causes and illustrate the Effects that they have.
- Create funny skits of April Fools' Day pranks.
- Discuss feelings and sensitivity and what an appropriate prank would be.
- Write stories about a prank that was played on you and share with the class.

Word Bank

joke
prank
laughter
harmless
funny
humorous
fool
errand
victim
silly

Children's Literature Ideas

Use for read-alouds, shared reading, silent reading, research, and so on.

Kroll, S. (1990). *It's April Fools' Day.* Holiday House, Inc. ISBN: 0823407470.

Maguire, G. (2004). *A Couple of April Fools.* Houghton Mifflin. ISBN: 061827474X.

Roy, R. (2003). *The School Skeleton.* Bantam Doubleday. ISBN: 0375813683.

Schiller, M. & Curry, D. (2003). *April Fools' Day.* Scholastic, Inc. ISBN: 0516279424.

Smith, G. (2004). *World's Greatest Practical Jokes.* Sterling Publishing, Co. ISBN: 1402710208.

Earth Day

Earth Day is a time for everyone to appreciate the beauty of planet Earth and to fight against pollution. Once a year, it is a great chance for all of us to come together and consider everything we have on our planet and what our planet gives to us. Earth Day provides us with the opportunity to talk about how we can keep Earth a beautiful place for everyone.

The first Earth Day was established by Senator Gaylord Nelson, a Democrat from Wisconsin, in 1970. He saw that very little was being done in government to address environmental issues and the impact of humans on the environment. He wanted to raise the awareness of fellow politi-

cians, so April 22 was set aside to recognize these global issues. The idea was a huge success with 20 million Americans participating in the very first Earth Day. This made politicians take notice! It continues to be a success to this day. We celebrate Earth Day on April 22 each year, and it is now celebrated in 140 nations around the globe.

Although it is officially celebrated one day each year, Earth Day must be taken seriously on a daily basis. As our natural resources begin to dwindle with time and global warming increases, it becomes more and more crucial that we take care of our Earth every day. In order to save our planet for future generations, we all need to do our part as well as continue to make sure our politicians are doing their part to address environmental issues. Some simple things we can all do include recycling, throwing our trash into appropriate receptacles, conserving energy by turning off lights not being used, planting trees, and carpooling. Every little bit helps!

| environment | reuse | pollution | park | animal |
| recycle | Earth | ocean | atmosphere | breathe |

Illustrate these four words:

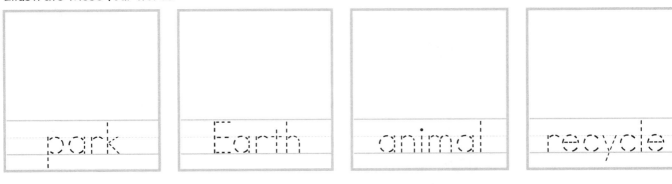

park   Earth   animal   recycle

Susan decided to do some recycling. In her recycling bin she put 3 newspapers, 6 bottles, and 7 cans. How many items has she recycled? Show your work.

Which one of these pictures shows what the Earth would look like from space? Circle it.

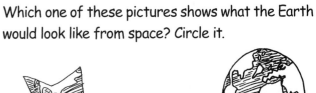

Draw what the Earth would look like as a flat map. List some of the characteristics of a map.

Draw a picture of what the Earth looks like as a round globe. List some characteristics of a globe.

Name: _____ Date: _____

environment	reuse	pollution	park	animal
recycle	Earth	ocean	atmosphere	breathe

Illustrate these four words:

park	*ocean*	*Earth*	*recycle*

At school, there are 90 cans on the playground. 3 children decided to pick up all the cans to recycle. Each child picked up an equal amount of cans. How many cans did each child get?

If you recycle and help keep the environment clean, which one of these things would not benefit? Circle it. Add one more item that would benefit from your help.

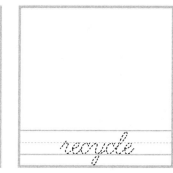

Draw things that can be recycled or conserved. Show yourself recycling these things.

Write the name of each item and how you can recycle or conserve it.

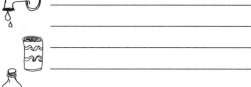
_____
_____
_____
_____
_____
_____
_____
_____
_____

Name: _____

Date: _____

Earth Day: Write about what is happening in the picture. What can you do to help the fish?

Name: _____   Date: _____

- -

Write about something that is polluting Earth. Add an illustration.

_____

_____

_____

_____

_____

_____

_____

_____

_____

_____

_____

_____

_____

_____

_____

Name: _____ Date: _____

· ·

Write about something you have done to help Earth.

_____

_____

_____

_____

_____

_____

_____

_____

_____

_____

_____

_____

_____

_____

Name:

Date:

Write about something you have done to help Earth.

Recycle Spinner

This is a great art project to help students remember what items they can recycle. Students practice telling other students about the items on their spinners and how the items are recycled. Be sure to copy the spinner templates onto heavy paper or cardstock.

Materials

scissors
spinner templates
brads
crayons

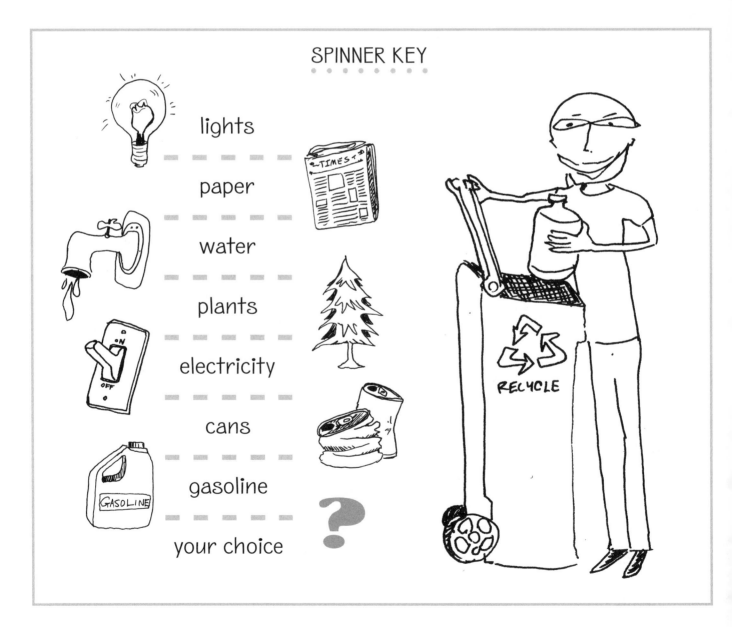

SPINNER KEY

lights

paper

water

plants

electricity

cans

gasoline

your choice

RECYCLE

Recycle Spinner

1. Cut out both templates.

2. After cutting out a template, each student can write the words of the recycle items, color the template, and write his or her name on it.

3. Connect the two together using a brad. Remember to cut out the windows of the top cover before connecting the two.

RECYCLE!

HELP ♻ EARTH

Spinner Template (Bottom)

water

plants

paper

electricity

lights

cans

?

gas

Earth Day Evergreen Tree Art

Make a classroom full of trees to help remind students to celebrate Earth Day every day! This is a fun activity that only requires green paper, scissors, and tape. But feel free to experiment with fancier trees, too!

Materials

2 sheets green construction paper
scissors
tape

1. Put both pieces of green paper together.

2. Fold paper in half.

3. Trace half of the tree as a guide for where to cut.

4. Cut out the tree traced on the paper.

5. Trace a guideline down the center of both trees.

6. Cut each tree only going halfway, one from the top and one from the bottom.

7. Make sure not to cut past the halfway point on each tree. If you want to write on the tree, do so now.

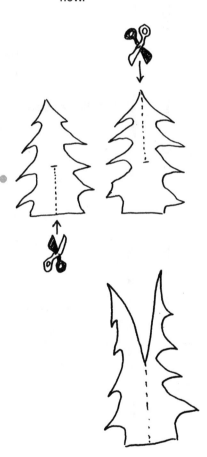

8. Slide both cut tree sections together.

9. The tree is finished and can be decorated.

Earth Day Puzzle: Copy this image onto colored card stock and laminate; then cut out the pieces. Place them in a self-sealing plastic bag for storage. Let the students put the puzzle together when they have free time. You may want to make four or five puzzles so students will have more than one to assemble.

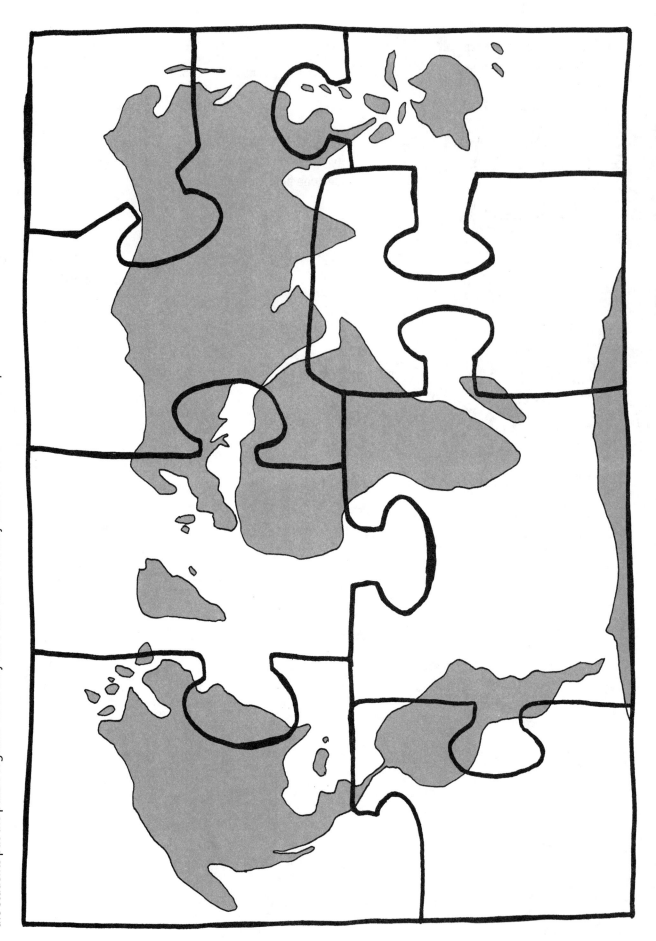

Earth Day Teacher Resource Page

Title

Colorful Border

Student Question

Rubric

Children's Work

Rubric Score/
Teacher Feedback

Teacher Example

State Standard

Lesson Extensions

- Graphic organizers are a great way for students to make connections between resources found on our planet and items in their everyday lives.
- Collect leaves—there are lots of things to do with them! They can be made into collages, they can be traced and colored, and they can be counted for a bar graph. The bar graph can be used as a bulletin board so that all the students can copy and record the data. Students' work can also be posted on the bulletin board with the graph and the leaves. You can have discussions on types of leaves and trees and expand this into all the resources we get from trees.
- Recycle, recycle, recycle! If you have a recycling program in your school, create posters to build awareness of it. If you don't have a recycling program, start one.

Word Bank

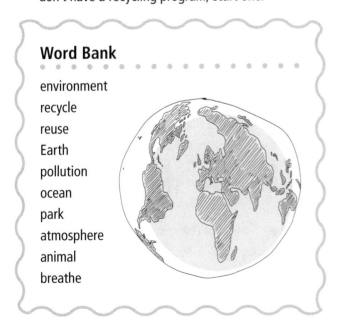

environment
recycle
reuse
Earth
pollution
ocean
park
atmosphere
animal
breathe

Children's Literature Ideas

Use for read-alouds, shared reading, silent reading, research, and so on.

Ansary, M. (2001). *Earth Day*. Heinemann Publishing. ISBN: 1588102203.

Cherry, L. (2000). *The Great Kapok Tree: A Tale of the Amazon Rain Forest*. Harcourt Brace. ISBN: 0152026142.

Hiaasen, C. (2004). *Hoot*. Knopf Publishing. ISBN: 0375829164.

Lowery, L. (2003). *Earth Day*. Lerner Publishing, Co. ISBN: 157505700X.

Nelson, R. (2003). *Earth Day*. Lerner Publishing, Co. ISBN: 0822512831.

Arbor Day

Arbor Day is celebrated each year on the last Friday in April in most states. It is an important holiday because it promotes tree planting and care. This holiday started in Nebraska in 1872. Many pioneers who settled the Nebraska Territory, a land of mostly plains and few trees, missed their trees. One such pioneer was J. Sterling Morton from Detroit. He found success as a journalist, eventually becoming editor of Nebraska's first newspaper, the *Nebraska City News*. He used this prominent position to spread the word about planting trees, and his message was well received. The pioneers missed their trees and needed trees to protect the soil from the wind. They also needed trees for fuel, shade, and building materials. Everyone was encouraged to participate in tree planting.

On January 4, 1872, Arbor Day was proposed by Morton, and the first Arbor Day was April 10, 1872. Prizes and incentives were offered for planting trees, and it is estimated that more than one million trees were planted on that first Arbor Day. A few years later, in 1874, Arbor Day became a legal holiday in Nebraska, and the date was set for April 22, Morton's birthday.

In the 1870s Arbor Day spread to other states. Today the holiday is even observed in other countries worldwide. Protecting our trees and forests has become a very important topic as we begin to run

low on natural resources. Recycling and reusing avoids the need to cut down more trees as paper, and paper goods can be made from recycled paper material. We have lost many trees, and our rain forests have been hit especially hard. We need to replenish those trees that have been cut down as well as maintain those trees in need of care.

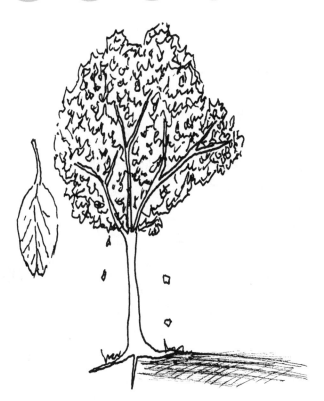

Deciduous
- Have leaves
- Lose leaves in cold or dry seasons

Coniferous (Evergreen)
- Have needles
- Stay green year-round

paper

fruit

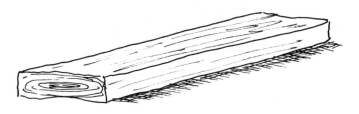

wood

Name: _____   Date: _____

| grow | branch | plant | root | deciduous |
| bark | leaf | trunk | limb | coniferous |

Illustrate these four words:

tree	leaf	root	branch

Trace these three words:

branches

trunk

roots

6 red leaves fell. Then 4 yellow leaves fell, and, finally, 3 orange leaves fell. How many leaves fell in all?

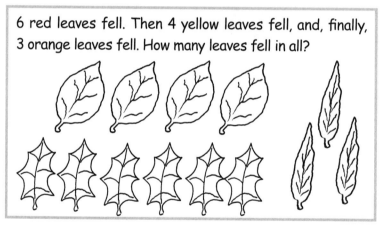

Trace these five words: trees

coniferous

needle

leaf

deciduous

Name: _____   Date: _____

Illustrate these four words:

deciduous   *limb*   *plant*   *coniferous*

10 deciduous trees each shed 14 leaves. How many leaves were shed in all?

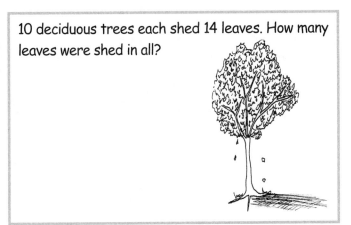

Label these types of trees.

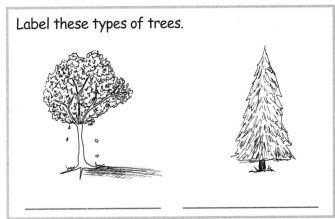

_____   _____

Parts of a Tree

trunk   branch   leaves   root

_____   _____

_____

_____

Tree Products   Fill in the blanks:

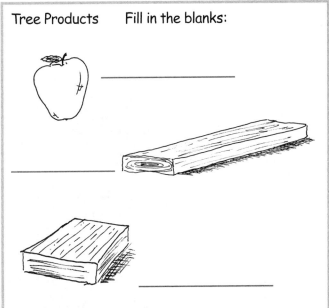

_____

_____

_____

Name: _____ Date: _____

Finish the drawing. Write about what you know of trees and how they help us.

_____

_____

_____

_____

Word Bank   grow   bark   branch   leaf   plant   trunk   root   limb   deciduous   coniferous

Name: Date:

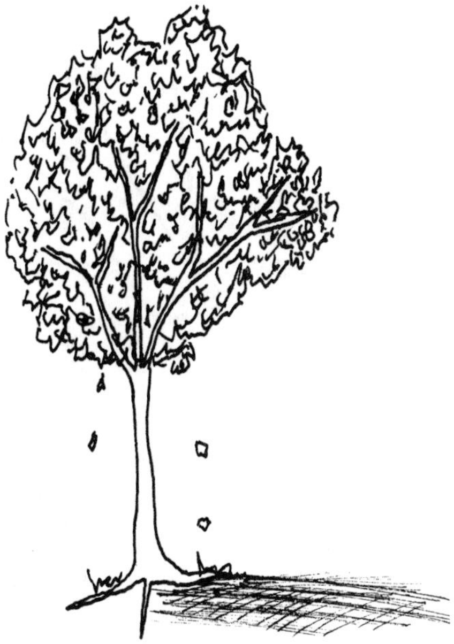

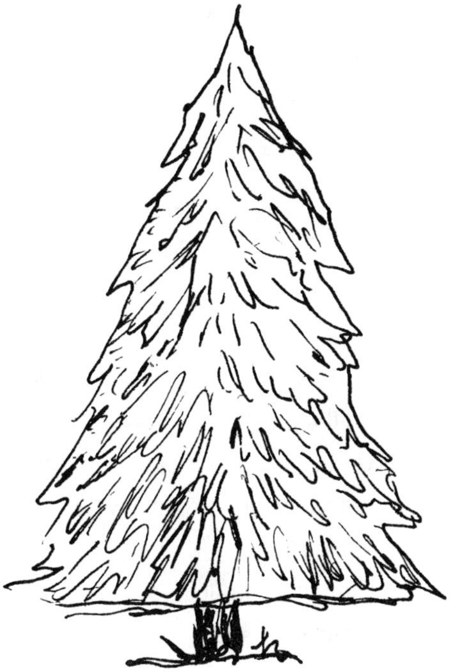

Finish illustrating the trees. Write what you know about trees and how you can help them.

Word Bank grow bark branch leaf plant trunk root limb deciduous coniferous

Word Tree

Materials

paper
glue
scissors
pencil

1. Write a word ending (phonogram) on the branch.
2. On the leaves, write words from the same family as the word ending.
3. Glue the word leaves to the branch.

Additional activities:

- Words beginning with the same letter
- Words with the same long vowel sound
- Words about the same theme (i.e., weather words)
- Words that describe characteristics of a person/character
- Words that categorize (e.g., things that fly)

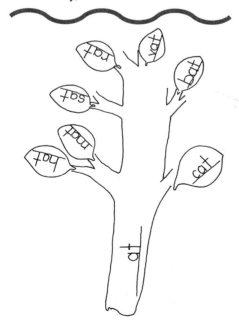

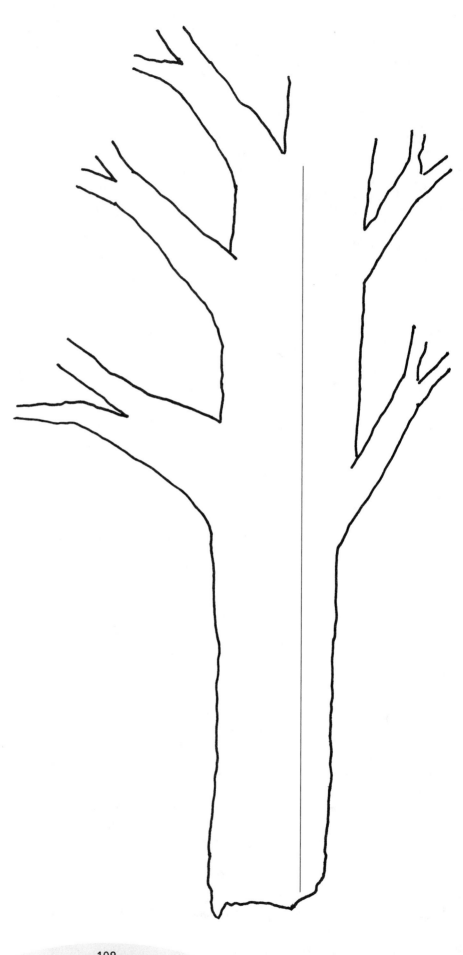

Word Tree

Story Tree

- Write about trees. How can you help to protect our trees?
- Write your ideas on the leaves and cut them out.
- Create a wall-sized tree with crumpled pieces of brown butcher paper or flat construction paper as branches.
- Attach leaves. Share.

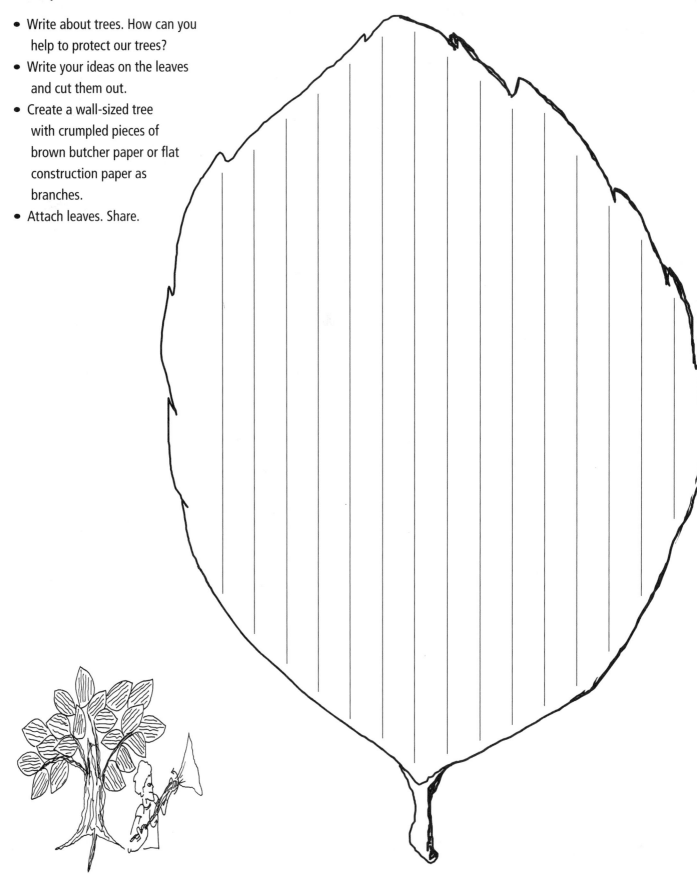

Arbor Day Teacher Resource Page

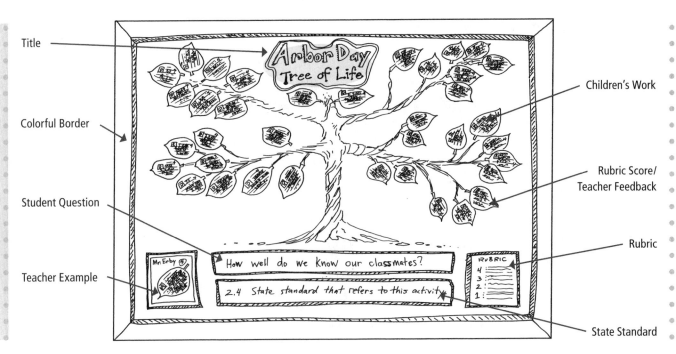

BULLETIN BOARD IDEA

Title

Colorful Border

Student Question

Teacher Example

Children's Work

Rubric Score/
Teacher Feedback

Rubric

State Standard

Arbor Day Tree of Life

How well do we know our classmates?

2.4 State standard that refers to this activity

RUBRIC
4
3
2
1

Lesson Extensions

- Create a Classroom Tree bulletin board using the leaf journal activity page.
- Contact a tree planting organization for a school visit.
- Plant trees on your school grounds.
- Make your own paper. There are many recipes available online.
- Recycle paper in the classroom by starting a scrap box for art projects. A good rule is to keep any scraps that are bigger than your hand and place them in the scrap box for use in future art projects.

Word Bank

grow
bark
branch
leaf
plant
trunk
root
limb
deciduous
coniferous

Children's Literature Ideas

Use for read-alouds, shared reading, silent reading, research, and so on.

Ansary, M. (2001). *Arbor Day.* Heinemann Publishers. ISBN: 158810219X.

Beaty, S., Wikerson, J., & Parkinson, J. (1999). *Champion of Arbor Day.* Acorn Books. ISBN: 0966447018.

Bennet, K. (2003). *Arbor Day.* Children's Press. ISBN: 0516228617.

Cooper, J. (2003). *Arbor Day.* Rourke Publishing, Inc. ISBN: 1589522176.

Reese, B. (1984). *Arbor Day.* ARO Publishing. ISBN: 089868031X.

May Day

The first of May is a popular holiday for many. In England long ago, people celebrated the end of winter and the beginning of spring by gathering flowers and greenery from the surrounding countryside on the first of May. This custom dates to the Romans, who honored their goddess of spring, Flora, and celebrated from April 28 to May 3, with the focus on May Day.

Another May Day tradition in England is the maypole. These tall poles are adorned with ribbons, streamers, flowers, and greenery. They are brightly painted and serve as the central point of the celebration. Children dance around the pole holding the loose ends of the ribbons that are attached to the top of the pole. As they dance in, out, and around the pole, children weave patterns with the ribbons. Some celebrations even select a May Queen.

Another May Day tradition is to decorate baskets, fill them with flowers, and leave them on the doorsteps of neighbors' homes. The purpose of this was originally to ensure fertility for the coming year, but today, it could just be an occasion to be nice to someone special. May baskets can include flowers, flower seeds, poetry, notes, letters, and even cookies or candy. They make excellent presents for the elderly, the sick, and those in need of uplifting or healing. They can offer support, bring a smile, and provide encouragement to their recipients.

In some countries May Day also serves as a Labor Day holiday. It is a day of parades, speeches, and occasional demonstrations. However you choose to work it into your curriculum, May Day is an excellent time to welcome spring and reflect on the beauty of nature during this time of year.

Name: _____ Date: _____

Illustrate these four words:

flower

queen

basket

ribbon

2 girls and 3 boys dance around the maypole. Then 4 more girls and 3 more boys join them. How many boys, girls, and students were there in all?

_____ girls

_____ boys

_____ total

Circle the items you would put in your May Day basket.

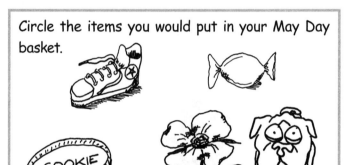

Finish the drawing. Add yourself and your friends dancing around the maypole.

Illustrate what you would add to a May Day basket.

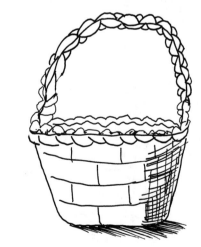

Word Bank

spring	greenery	maypole	streamer	basket
flower	flora	ribbon	queen	celebration

Illustrate these four words:

flower	*queen*	*basket*	*ribbon*

A total of 15 boys and 21 girls took turns dancing around the maypole. Everyone danced 1 dance. If there were 3 turns with the same amount of boys and girls in each turn, how many boys and girls danced each turn? What was the ratio of boys to girls for each dance?

Boys: _____
Girls: _____
Ratio: _____:_____

Write a May Day note for a May Day basket.

Happy May Day!

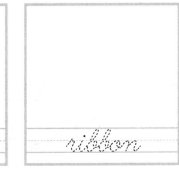

Finish drawing the maypole. Draw you and your friends.

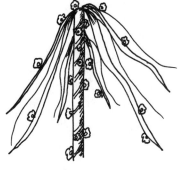

Illustrate what you would add to a May Day basket.

Name: _____

Date: _____

Write about how you would like to celebrate May Day.
Draw you and your friends around the maypole.

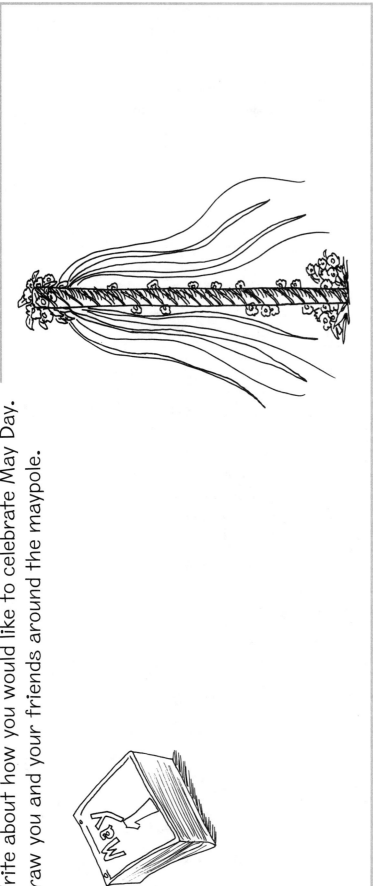

_____

_____

_____

Word Bank   spring   flower   greenery   flora   maypole   ribbon   streamer   queen   basket   celebration

Name: _____   Date: _____

Write about how you would celebrate May
Day. Draw you and your
friends around the maypole.

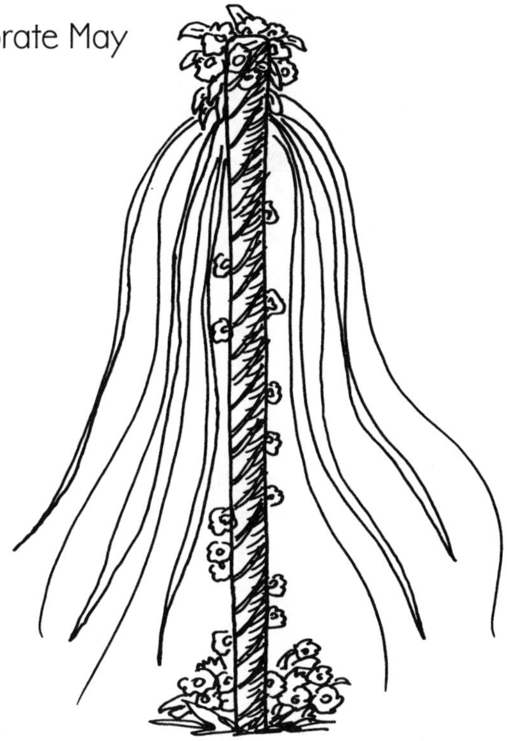

_____

_____

_____

_____

_____

_____

_____

_____

_____

_____

_____

_____

Word Bank   spring flower greenery flora maypole ribbon streamer queen basket celebration

May Day Basket

Students can create their own mini May Day basket; fill it basket with candies, cookies, or flowers; and attach a note and leave it for a special friend.

Materials

glue
scissors
crayons
hole punch
pipe cleaner

1. Color and label box (Happy May Day, etc.).
2. Cut out, fold, and glue the box.
3. Punch a hole in each side. Connect a pipe cleaner handle.
4. Fill the basket and deliver.

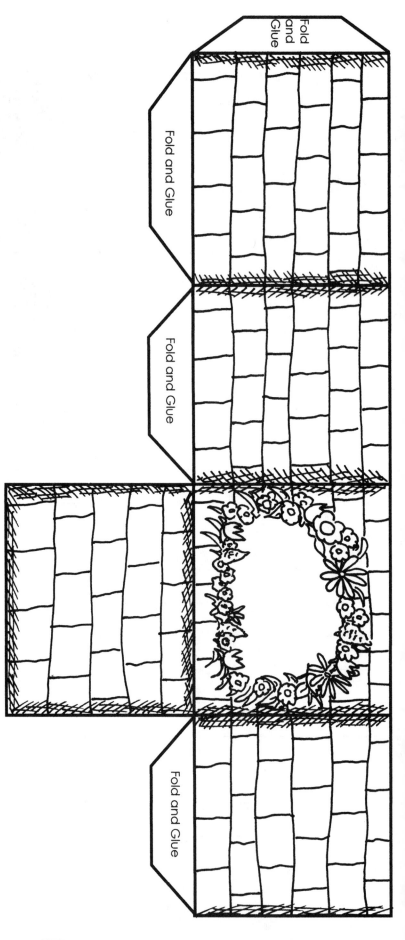

May Day Teacher Resource Page

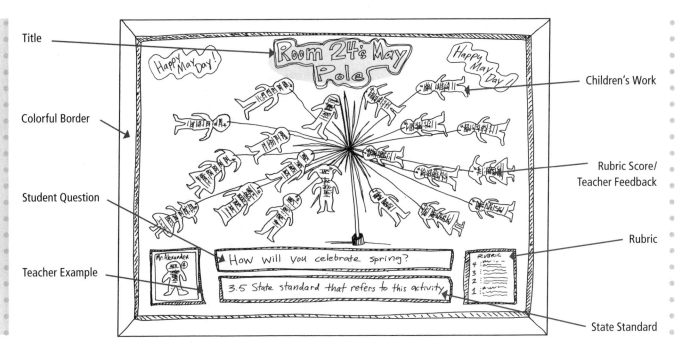

Title

Colorful Border

Student Question

Teacher Example

Children's Work

Rubric Score/
Teacher Feedback

Rubric

State Standard

How will you celebrate spring?

3.5 State standard that refers to this activity

Lesson Extensions

- Create a May Day Maypole bulletin board with student journals around the pole. Students should write about how they will celebrate spring.
- Create a real maypole with ribbons and streamers, and have students dance around it.
- Create May baskets to deliver around the school.
- Study flowers and seeds. Plant flowers, and discuss seed germination. Measure growth of plants and roots.
- Study Vincent van Gogh, Georgia O'Keeffe, Claude Monet, and other artists who have painted flowers. Then have students paint their own flowers.

Word Bank

spring
flower
greenery
flora
maypole
ribbon
streamer
queen
basket
fertility

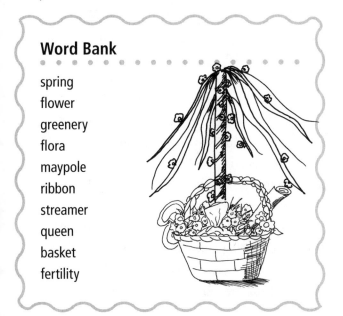

Children's Literature Ideas

Use for read-alouds, shared reading, silent reading, research, and so on.

Berger, S. & Chanko, P. (2003). *It's Spring!* Scholastic, Inc. ISBN: 0439442389.

Butterfield, M. (2005). *Spring.* Smart Apple Media. ISBN: 158340614X.

Carr, J. (2002). *Splish, Splash, Spring.* Holiday House, Inc. ISBN: 0823417549.

Early, J. (2006). *Spring.* Gareth Stevens Audio. ISBN: 0836863542.

Schutte, S. (2007). *Let's Look at Spring.* Pebble Plus. ISBN: 0736867074.

Cinco de Mayo

Cinco de Mayo is Spanish for the "fifth of May." That is an important date that marks the victory of the Mexican army over the French at the *Batalla de Puebla* ("Battle of Puebla") in 1862. Although the Mexican army was eventually defeated in the war, this battle became an important symbol of Mexican unity and patriotism. The victory in the Battle of Puebla was the turning point that showed the world that Mexico and other Latin American countries were willing to defend themselves against foreign forces.

The years leading up to the *Batalla de Puebla* were full of turmoil in Mexico. The Mexican-American War (1846–1848) and the Mexican Civil War of 1858 had taken their toll on the economy. Mexico was struggling to repay debts to Spain, England, and France. President Benito Juarez declared that Mexico would stop repaying all foreign debt for two years in order to give the country time to rebuild its economy. In 1861 Spain, England, and France decided they needed to invade Mexico to reclaim the money owed to them. France saw this as an opportunity to expand its empire and take control. Spain and England, aware of France's plans, withdrew.

The French, under Napoleon III, continued forward with their plan and invaded Mexico in 1862 along the Gulf Coast at Veracruz and began to advance on to Mexico City. The French army, however, met resistance along the way at the city of Puebla. General Ignacio Zaragoza led a small army of only 5,000 Mestizo and Zapotec Indians to battle the French. His army was small and not nearly as well armed as the French. Miraculously, however, his forces defeated the French army in the Batalla de Puebla on May 5, 1862. This showed the world that Mexico was willing to fight for its independence.

May 5 is *not* Mexico's Independence Day as many often confuse it. Mexico's Independence Day actually happened almost 50 years later on September 16, 1810. Cinco de Mayo is more of a regional holiday in Mexico, especially in the state of Puebla, and it has become a more prominent holiday in the United States through time. Through the years, the celebration of the victory at the Batalla de Puebla has come to be known simply as Cinco de Mayo. In the United States, Mexican-Americans celebrate with festivities, concerts, parties, and traditional Mexican dancing and customs. Children sometimes wear traditional clothing—often in the red, white, and green colors of the Mexican flag—and perform traditional Mexican dances. The Cinco de Mayo celebration in the United States also has grown to emphasize the link between the two countries, with many people enjoying a variety of activities.

Name: _____   Date: _____

| celebrate | party | Mexico | festival | Spanish |
| victory | May | French | English | parade |

Illustrate these four words:

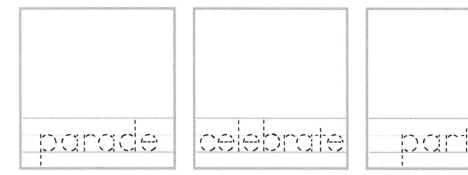

parade   celebrate   party   festival

Nick made 5 blue paper flowers for Cinco de Mayo. Eloisa made 4 yellow flowers. Jay made 6 red flowers. Ruben made 2 maracas. How many flowers were made in all?

Color the maracas. Circle the maraca that doesn't belong.

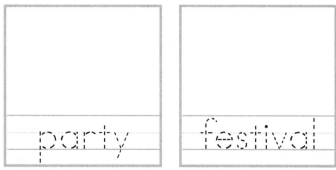

Draw a design on the maraca and color it.

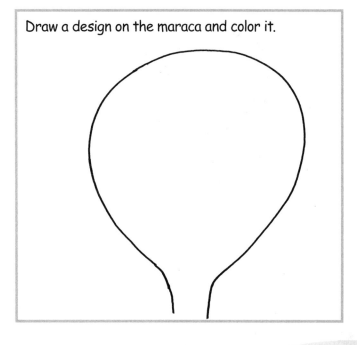

Spanish Numbers

1	one	uno
2	two	dos
3	three	tres
4	four	cuatro
5	five	cinco
6	six	seis
7	seven	siete
8	eight	ocho
9	nine	nueve
10	ten	diez

Name: _____ Date: _____

| celebrate | party | Mexico | festival | Spanish |
| victory | May | French | English | parade |

Illustrate these four words:

celebrate

parade

festival

victory

Each class made paper flowers to decorate the school for Cinco de Mayo. There were 15 classes. 5 classes had 22 students, 3 classes had 24 students, and 7 classes had 25 students. 30 students made red flowers. How many flowers were made in all?

History

The battle of _____ was the defeat of the _____ by a small Mexican army led by _____. This battle showed the world that Mexico was willing to fight for its independence. It took _____ years to gain independence. Mexico gained its independence on _____.

Mexican Coat of Arms

Color and label the serpent, eagle, and cactus.

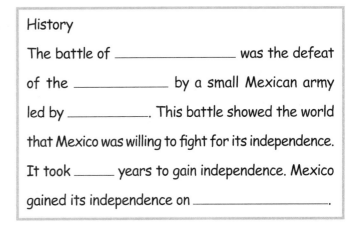

_____

_____

_____

How long is the maraca?

_____ in.

_____ cm

_____ mm

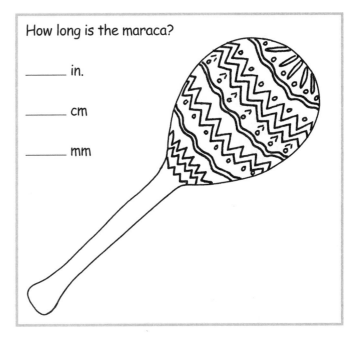

Name: _____

Date: _____

Write about and illustrate the
history of Cinco de Mayo.

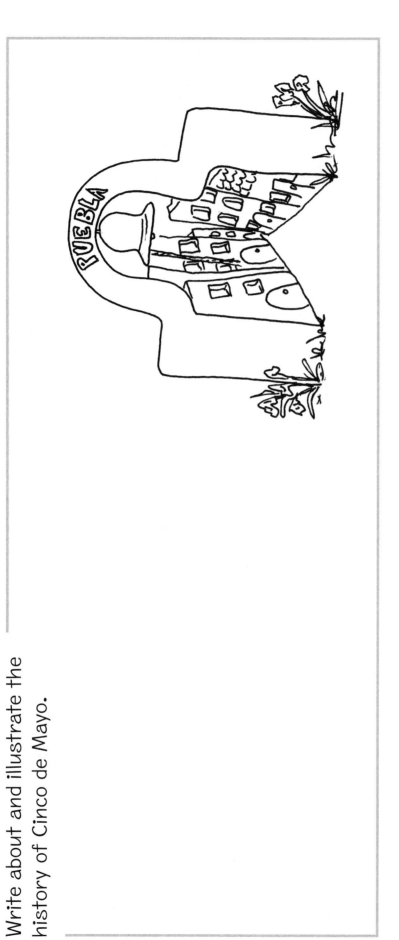

_____

_____

_____

_____

Word Bank   celebrate   victory   party   May   Mexico   French   festival   English   Spanish   parade

Name: _____ Date: _____

Write about and illustrate the history of Cinco de Mayo.

_____

_____

_____

_____

_____

_____

_____

_____

_____

_____

_____

_____

_____

Word Bank   celebrate   victory   party   May   Mexico   French   festival   English   Spanish   parade

The Mexican Flag

Mexico's national flag was created in 1821 after Mexico won its independence from Spain. Today's flag is the fourth variation. The image in the center is slightly different from the original flag, but the general design remains the same. The flag features three evenly sized panels of green, white, and red. Each color means something: green represents hope, white represents purity, and red represents the blood of national heroes. The center of the flag features the Mexican coat of arms: an eagle perched on a cactus holding a serpent in its talon. This icon comes from an Aztec legend in which gods tell the Aztec people to build a city on the location where they find an eagle with a serpent in its talon while perched on a pear cactus. After many years of wandering, the Aztecs finally found the described eagle on Lake Texcoco and built their new capital, Tenochtitlán, there. Tenochtitlán later became Mexico City, the modern-day capital of Mexico.

Mexican Flag Art

Create your own Mexican flag. Cut out the flag. Color the coat of arms. Cut out small squares of red and green tissue paper (approximately 2″ × 2″). Use a pencil eraser to crumple the tissue paper squares. Glue the red on the left side of the flag and the green on the right side of the flag.

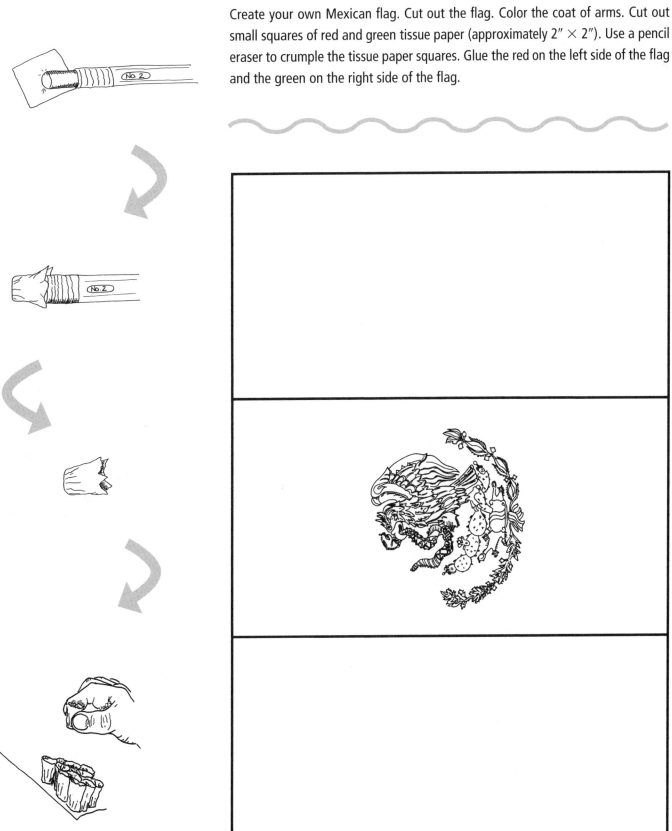

Green

White

Red

Cinco de Mayo Mexican Paper Flowers

One of the most popular Cinco de Mayo decorations used at parties and in parades is the Mexican paper flower. It's fun and easy to make.

Materials

pipe cleaner
tissue paper
scissors

1. Cut 4–8 rectangles of colored tissue paper (4″ × 6″).

2. Stack the rectangles.

3. Fold the stack, as if to make a fan, starting with the longer side.

4. Cut two small notches in the center on each side to wrap the pipe cleaner around.

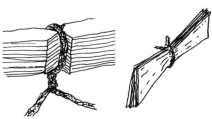

5. Wrap a pipe cleaner around the middle at the notches of the fan-folded paper and twist a few times, leaving the ends for securing your flower in place later.

6. Carefully pull apart the tissue papers one at a time, pulling toward the center (the pipe cleaner) and separating the paper along the way.

7. Slightly crimp and fluff along the way to create a full flower.

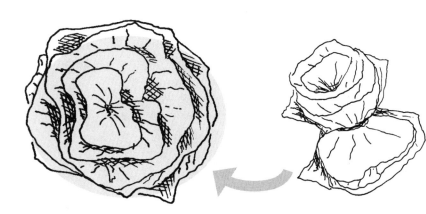

Cinco de Mayo Teacher Resource Page

BULLETIN BOARD IDEA

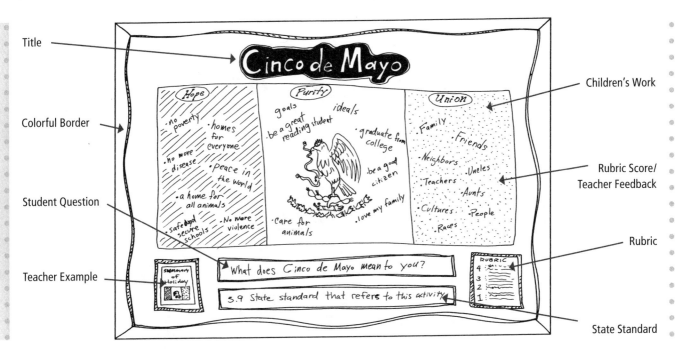

Title

Colorful Border

Student Question

Teacher Example

Children's Work

Rubric Score/
Teacher Feedback

Rubric

State Standard

Cinco de Mayo

Hope · *Purity* · *Union*

- no poverty
- homes for everyone
- no more disease
- peace in the world
- a home for all animals
- safe and secure schools
- No more violence

goals · ideals
be a great reading student
graduate from college
be a good citizen
love my family
care for animals

Family · Friends
Neighbors · Uncles
Teachers · Aunts
Cultures · People
Races

What does Cinco de Mayo mean to you?

5.9 State standard that refers to this activity

RUBRIC 4 3 2 1

summary of holiday

Lesson Extensions

- Assign a research paper, including a time line, about the history of Cinco de Mayo. Students can use textbooks, the Internet, and nonfiction picture books.
- Create the various traditional decorations, such as tissue paper with cut-out designs and altars described in many of the available children's picture books.

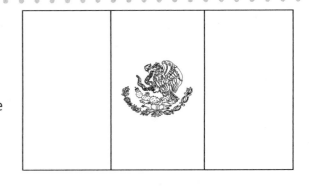

Word Bank

celebrate
victory
party
May
Mexico
French
festival
English
Spanish
parade

Children's Literature Ideas

Use for read-alouds, shared reading, silent reading, research, and so on.

Garcia, A. (2003). *Cinco de Mayo.* Heinemann Library. ISBN: 140343686X.

Lawery, L. (2005). *Cinco de Mayo.* Lerner Publishing Group. ISBN: 1575056542.

Murray, J. (2005). *Cinco de Mayo.* ABDO Publishing. ISBN: 1591975867.

Urrutia, M. & Orozco, R. (2002). *Cinco de Mayo: Yesterday and Today.* Ground Wood Books. ISBN: 0888994842.

Vazquez, S. (1998). *Cinco de Mayo.* Raintree Publishers. ISBN: 0817255621.

Mother's Day

How do you and your mother and/or grand-mother celebrate Mother's Day? Do you go to breakfast, take a trip to the mall, play outside, go to the beach or the park, or have dinner as a family? Why is this day so important?

Mother's Day can be traced back to several origins. Some trace it back to the Greek spring cele-brations of Rhea, the mother of the gods. In England, during the 1600s, mothers were honored on "Moth-ering Sunday," celebrated on the fourth Sunday of Lent. On this day servants were also given the day off to spend time honoring their mothers.

In the United States, Mother's Day was initially proposed by Julia Ward Howe in 1872. She held annual Mother's Day meetings in Boston, Massachusetts. It was a day dedicated to peace, but it never became an official holiday. Later, in 1907, Ana Jarvis proposed celebrating a memo-rial day for women called Mother's Day. The date was set for the second Sunday in May in memory of the anniversary of the death of her mother, a strong advocate and organizer of women during the Civil War.

On May 10, 1908, the first Mother's Day was held in Ana Jarvis's church. From there it spread to other communities and states. By 1912, some states were calling it an official holi-day. Then, in 1914, President Woodrow Wilson made Mother's Day a national holiday to be held each year on the second Sunday of May.

Countries around the world celebrate Mother's Day in their own unique ways. Many countries celebrate Mother's Day throughout the year. Some countries, including Australia, Belgium, Denmark, Finland, Italy, and Turkey, celebrate it on the same day in May as the United States.

This worldwide celebration of mothers shows how important we all believe mothers are. So on Mother's Day, show your appreciation to whomever you call Mom.

Name: _____   Date: _____

Illustrate these four words:

What fractions of the flowers in the vase are shaded?

Which one of these people would not get a Mother's Day card? Circle that person.

List five things that make your mother great!

1. _____

2. _____

3. _____

4. _____

5. _____

Draw a bouquet of flowers for your mom.

Name: _____   Date: _____

| Sunday | Mom | aunt | card | appreciate |
| Grandma | May | sister | gift | love |

Illustrate these four words:

Sunday	*Grandma*	*appreciate*	*sister*

The flower shop has 245 flowers. They buy 185 more flowers for Mother's Day. They then find 2 more flowers in a box under the table. If they put 18 flowers in each bouquet, how many bouquets can the flower shop make?

Draw and label the three things necessary to grow flowers.

Using flowers, design a Mother's Day card.

Write down and illustrate two things you will do for your mom on Mother's Day.

Name:

Date:

Write about how you plan to celebrate Mother's Day.

Word Bank   Sunday   Grandma   Mom   May   aunt   sister   card   gift   appreciate   love

Name: _____   Date: _____

Happy Mother's Day! Write about how you plan to celebrate Mother's Day.

Mother's Day Gift Box

Materials

glue
scissors
crayons
copies of template for each student

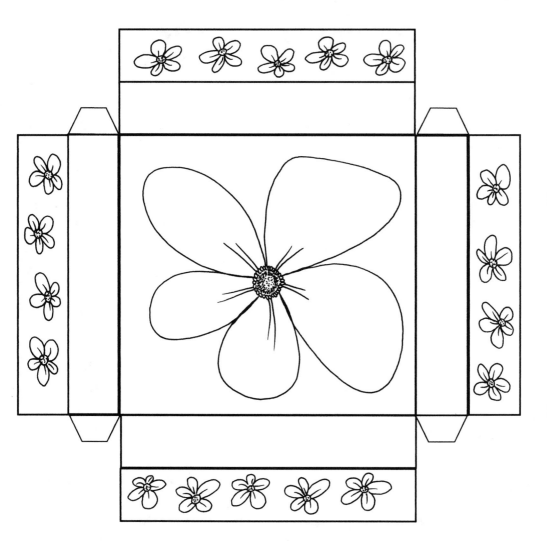

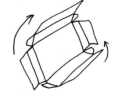

1. Have students cut out the template, color, and decorate it.

2. Pre-fold all lines and then glue the tabs on the outside of the box first.

3. After gluing the tabs, fold over the flaps and glue them down, hiding the tabs.

4. Students can present the box to Mom on her special day.

136

Mother's Day Teacher Resource Page

Title

Colorful Border

Student Question

Teacher Example

Children's Work

Rubric Score/
Teacher Feedback

Rubric

State Standard

Labels within bulletin board: Sunflower Field · Mother's Day! · Mothers help us to bloom! · What makes your Mother special? · 1.4 State standard that refers to this lesson. · RUBRIC 4 3 2 1

Lesson Extensions

- Create a Field of Sunflower Journals bulletin board. Have students reflect on their mother or mother figure and what makes that person special.
- Create a photo collage of mothers or famous mothers. Have students write about their mother or a famous mother.
- Have a Mother's Tea by inviting mothers into the classroom for a celebration.
- Invite mothers to come read or volunteer in the classroom.
- Draw or paint portraits of mothers.

Word Bank

Sunday
Grandma
Mom
May
aunt
sister
card
gift
appreciate
love

Children's Literature Ideas

Use for read-alouds, shared reading, silent reading, research, and so on.

Evans, E. (2001). *I Love You Mommy!* Golden Books. ISBN: 0307995070.

Joosse, B. (1991). *Mama, Do You Love Me?* Chronicle Books LLC. ISBN: 087701759X.

Memed, L. (1998). *I Love You as Much.* HarperCollins. ISBN: 0688159788.

Parr, T. (2002). *The Mommy Book.* Little, Brown and Co. ISBN: 0316608270.

Rockwell, A. (2004). *Mother's Day.* HarperCollins. ISBN: 0060513748.

Victoria Day

Canadians love to celebrate Victoria Day, a celebration known for its spectacular fireworks displays that take place across the country. Victoria Day is a time for family and friends to get together. They may take boat cruises, go on picnics in the park, or check out local celebrations. So just what is Victoria Day?

Victoria Day celebrates the birth of Queen Victoria on May 24. She was the reigning monarch when Canada was under British rule from 1837 to 1901. Even after Canada became an independent nation in 1867, most Canadians remained loyal to their queen, and after her death in 1901 her birthday was declared a national holiday. Victoria Day celebrations have continued throughout the years, and the day is also celebrated in England and Scotland. Canadians celebrate Victoria Day on the Monday before May 25, while England and parts of Scotland celebrate sometime in early June. Today, no matter who the British monarch is, his or her birthday is also celebrated on Victoria Day.

Canadians love this three-day weekend that unofficially welcomes summer. Many summer businesses open on this weekend, and preparation for the summer begins. So in all the excitement of summer approaching, don't forget to wish the monarch a happy birthday!

138

Name: _____ Date: _____

Illustrate these four words:

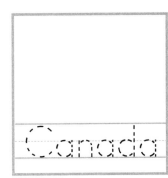

The queen's crown has 42 emerald diamonds. It also has 24 purple diamonds. How many diamonds does the crown have altogether?

What does Victoria Day celebrate?

Make a card for the queen's birthday.

Draw a crown on the queen's head, and then color the picture.

Name: _____   Date: _____

Illustrate these four words:

Victoria

Ontario

reign

national

The crown maker needs 42 rubies that cost $2,150 each. She also needs 8 diamonds that cost $3,900 each. Finally, she needs $5,215 to add gold to the crown. When she is finished making the crown, what will the total cost be?

Circle the person celebrated on Victoria Day.

List five people the Queen of England might invite to her birthday celebration!

1. _____

2. _____

3. _____

4. _____

5. _____

Design a crown to be worn by the queen.

Name:

Date:

Describe what you've learned about Victoria Day.

Word Bank   queen   birthday   Canada   tradition   national   Victoria   celebrate   monarch   reign   spring

Happy Victoria Day!

Describe what you've learned about Victoria Day.

Queen's Crown

List five things that you have learned about Victoria Day.

fold

fold

Victoria Day Teacher Resource Page

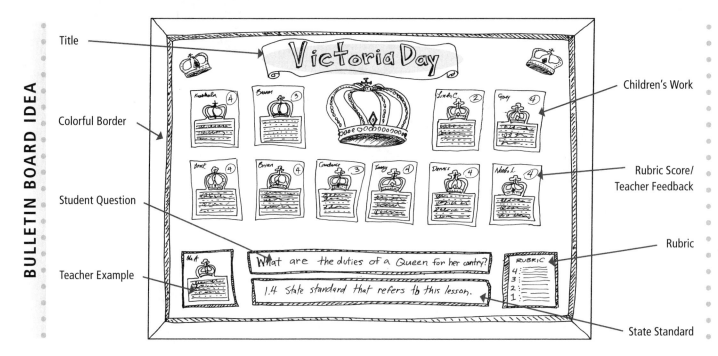

Title

Colorful Border

Student Question

Teacher Example

Children's Work

Rubric Score/
Teacher Feedback

Rubric

State Standard

Lesson Extensions

- Mount students' crown activities onto construction paper and display on a bulletin board.
- Watch a documentary on the British monarchy.
- Have students do research projects on selected members of the British monarchy throughout history.
- Write letters or send cards to the Queen of England.

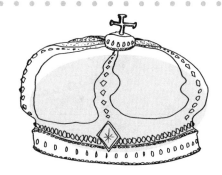

Word Bank

queen
birthday
Canada
tradition
national
Victoria
celebrate
monarch
reign
spring

Children's Literature Ideas

Use for read-alouds, shared reading, silent reading, research, and so on.

Kalman, B. & Walker, N. (1999). *Canada from A to Z.* Crabtree Publishing. ISBN: 0865054118.

Kalman, B. (2001). *Canada the Culture.* Crabtree Publishing. ISBN: 0778797287.

Landau, E. (2000). *Canada.* Scholastic, Inc. ISBN: 0516270214.

Little, C. (2003). *What's It Like to Live in Canada?* School Specialty Children's Publishing. ISBN: 1577688783.

Moore, C. (2002). *The Big Book of Canada: Exploring the Provinces and Territories.* Tundra Publishing. ISBN: 0887764576.

Ulmer, M. (2004). *M Is for Maple: A Canadian Alphabet.* Thompson Gale Publishing. ISBN: 1585362352.

Memorial Day

How do you remember those who have served their country in war? Remembering those people who have sacrificed and even given their lives for their country is important. In the United States, Memorial Day is a special day of remembrance each year when we honor U.S. soldiers who died fighting for their country. Their sacrifices have guaranteed the liberty, freedom, and privileges the rest of us enjoy.

Memorial Day originated in 1868 when Union General John A. Logan proposed a day where the graves of Civil War soldiers would be visited and decorated. This day was called Decoration Day. A few decades later, the name was changed to Memorial Day and it became a day dedicated to all soldiers who had given their lives. In 1971, the U.S. Congress declared it a national holiday, and we now celebrate Memorial Day on the last Monday of May each year.

Remembering the honor, spirit, and dedication of those who sacrificed their lives for our freedom is the purpose of Memorial Day. Many observe it by visiting cemeteries and placing a flag or some flowers on the grave of a soldier.

In addition, many people have the day off from work and school, and this three-day weekend has traditionally become a time for barbecues and picnics with family and friends to unofficially welcome summer. Despite all the fun that it can bring, it's important to keep in mind what this day represents since we all benefit from the sacrifices of such brave men and women.

Word Bank

honor	country	war	grave	flag
serve	remember	memorial	soldier	brave

Illustrate these four words:

soldier

grave

flag

brave

Kristen, Ben, James, and Charlie went to the cemetery to place flags on the graves of soldiers on Memorial Day. Kristen placed 24 flags, and each of the boys placed 10. How many flags were placed in all?

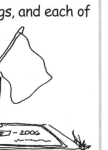

Which one is a memorial? Circle it.

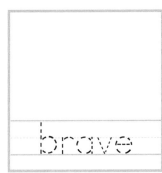

Dr. K Becker
PEDIATRICIAN

Draw a memorial that you would create to honor those soldiers who sacrificed their lives for their country.

Write three responsibilities of a soldier.

1. _____

2. _____

3. _____

Name: Date:

Word Bank

| honor | country | war | grave | flag |
| serve | remember | memorial | soldier | brave |

Illustrate these four words:

soldier	*grave*	*flag*	*brave*

A group of Boy Scouts visited the cemetery to place flags on soldiers' graves. 10 boys had 30 flags each, 5 boys had 15 flags each, and 3 boys had 25 flags each. They placed all but 13 of the flags. How many flags were placed in all?

What is the purpose of a memorial?

_____
_____
_____
_____
_____
_____

Draw a memorial that you would create to honor soldiers who sacrificed their lives for the country.

List three memorials dedicated to the fallen soldiers of our country.

1. _____

2. _____

3. _____

Name:

Date:

Write about and illustrate how you will remember those who have fought for our freedom. Finish our flag.

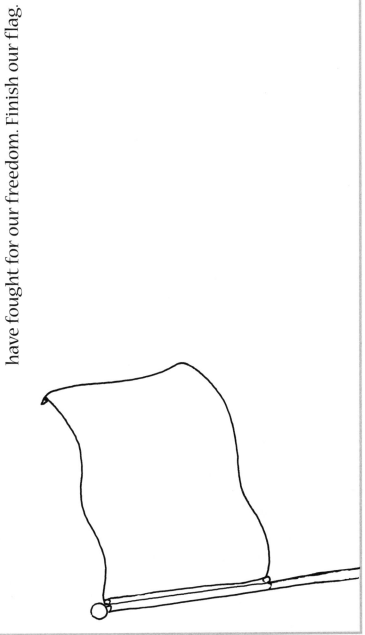

Word Bank   honor   serve   country   remember   war   memorial   grave   soldier   flag   brave

Name: _____   Date: _____

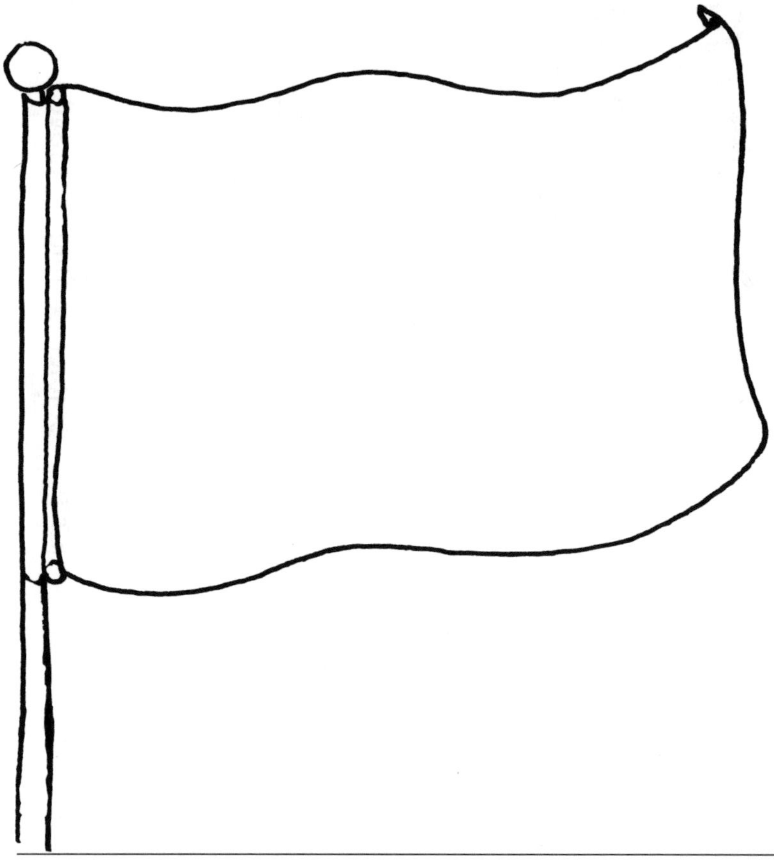

Write about and illustrate how you will remember those who have fought for our freedom. Finish our flag.

_____
_____
_____
_____
_____
_____
_____
_____
_____
_____

Word Bank   honor   serve   country   remember   war   memorial   grave   soldier   flag   brave

Memorial Day Pinwheel

Materials

pinwheel template
scissors
crayons
pencil
pushpin

1. Cut out the square and decorate it with colors and symbols from the flag.
2. Fold along the diagonal lines.
3. Cut halfway down each diagonal line (to the solid line) from the corners toward the center.
4. Fold every other corner to the center and attach.
5. Pin wheel to a pencil eraser with a pushpin.
6. Wave the pinwheel in a breeze and enjoy!

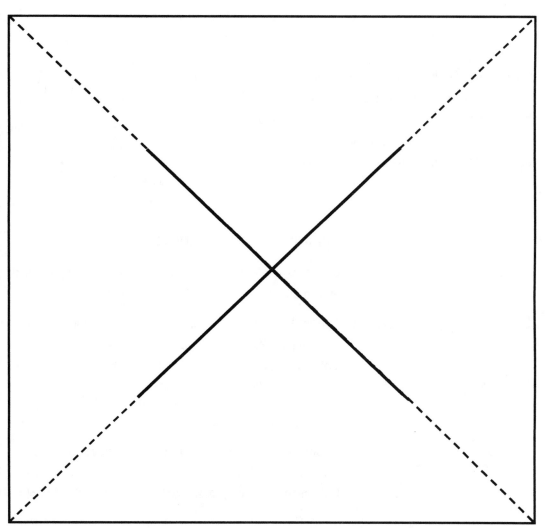

Memorial Day Teacher Resource Page

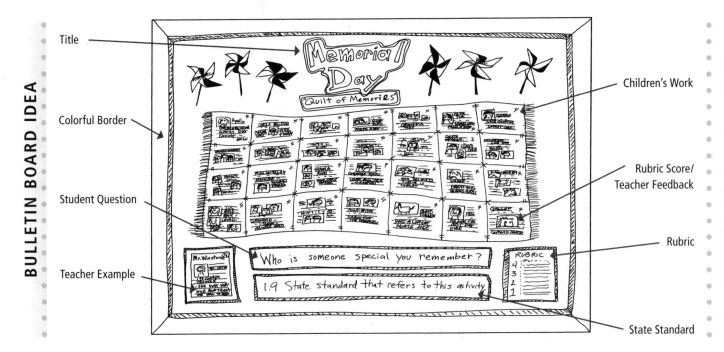

Title

Colorful Border

Student Question

Teacher Example

Children's Work

Rubric Score/
Teacher Feedback

Rubric

State Standard

Who is someone special you remember?

1.9 State standard that refers to this activity

Lesson Extensions

- Create a Memorial Day memory quilt. Students can journal about someone special, and the journals can be tied or glued together into a quilt. Display on the bulletin board.
- Have students write a letter to a person in the military, thanking them for their bravery so that we can continue to experience our freedoms in the United States.
- As a class, prepare care packages to be sent to the troops overseas.

Word Bank

honor
serve
country
remember
war
memorial
grave
soldier
flag
brave

Children's Literature Ideas

Use for read-alouds, shared reading, silent reading, research, and so on.

Cotton, J. (2002). *Memorial Day.* Scholastic Library Publishing. ISBN: 0516273698.

Golding, T. (2004). *Memorial Day Surprise.* Boyds Mills Press. ISBN: 1590780485.

Hamilton, L. (2004). *Memorial Day.* Weigh Publishers, Inc. ISBN: 1590361059.

Nelson, R. (2002). *Memorial Day.* Lerner Publishing Group. ISBN: 082251317X.

Nobleman, M. (2004). *Memorial Day.* Compass Point Books. ISBN: 0756507715.

Canada Day

Canada Day marks the anniversary of the day that the dominion of the British North American provinces and territories merged to form the federation known as Canada. The holiday has evolved over time. It was established in 1879 as Dominion Day and was officially celebrated in 1917 for the 50th anniversary of the confederation. In 1958 the Canadian government established an annual observance of the day, and in 1968, the celebration started to include more activities. Multicultural and professional concerts, sporting events, and artistic events began to take prominence, and soon this celebration became known as the "Festival of Canada." It extended the entire month of July and was held in the National Capital region.

In 1980, the celebrations spread to cities and communities throughout Canada. Canada's birthday started being celebrated in a big way, with 15 major cities holding fireworks displays.

As the celebrations continued to grow in size and importance to Canada, on October 27, 1982, Dominion Day officially became Canada Day. Canada now celebrates its birthday on July 1, and each province plans it own Canada Day celebration. These celebrations typically include entertainment with a Canadian theme, fireworks, and even pancake breakfasts. The Canadian flag flies high. This is a patriotic opportunity for Canadian communities to come together and celebrate their country and unity. By celebrating the accomplishments of famous Canadians from all walks of life, Canada Day gives Canadians a sense of pride.

Name: _____   Date: _____

Illustrate these four words:

 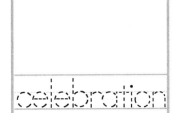  

festival   celebration   flag   fireworks

There were 15 pancakes on the plate. Greg ate 4 of the pancakes, Pam ate 3, and Dave ate 5. How many pancakes were left on the plate?

This is North America. Find Canada on the map, and color it red.

Draw the national symbol of Canada.

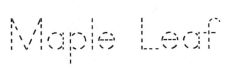

Maple Leaf

Canada

Name: _____   Date: _____

Illustrate these four words:

flag

celebration

concert

festival

Pancake breakfasts for Canada Day celebrations cost $3.00 each. If 50 breakfasts are served, how much money was collected? If the total cost for the ingredients was $37.45, what was the profit?

This is North America. Find Canada, and color it red. Color the United States blue. Color Mexico green. Color Greenland yellow. These are the four largest North American countries.

Draw and color the Canadian flag.

Colors: _____ and _____
Symbol: _____

156

Name: _____

Date: _____

Write about Canada Day. Tell how you would celebrate Canada Day. Illustrate.

Word Bank   Canada   province   territory   dominion   celebration   festival   patriotic   flag   concert   North America

Name: _____   Date: _____

Write about Canada Day. How would you celebrate Canada Day? Illustrate.

_____

_____

_____

_____

_____

_____

_____

_____

_____

_____

_____

_____

Word Bank   Canada province territory dominion celebration festival patriotic flag concert North America

Canadian Flag

Making a Canadian flag is an excellent way to celebrate Canada Day!

Materials

crayons
glue
scissors
Popsicle stick or
  coffee stirrer

1. Have students color both sides of the Canadian flag—red on each side with a red maple leaf in the center.

2. Cut out the flag.

3. Fold in half and glue a Popsicle stick or coffee stirrer in the fold.

4. Glue halves together.

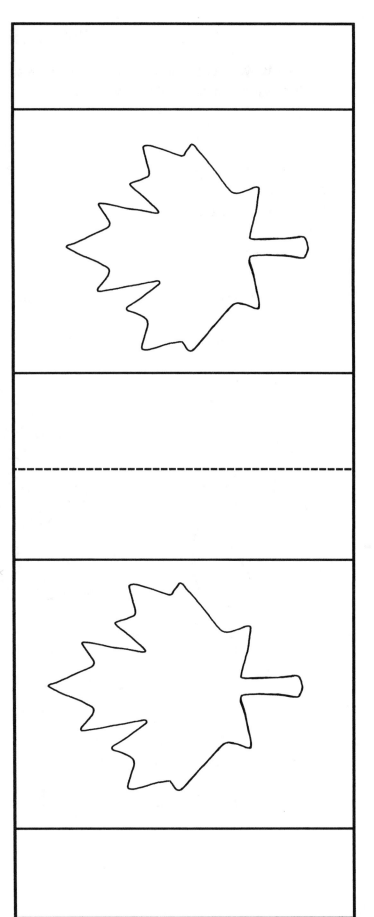

Map of Canada

Canada has two types of geographic regions: provinces and territories. Students will research and then color the 10 provinces and three territories of Canada.

Provinces

- ☐ Alberta
- ☐ British Columbia
- ☐ Manitoba
- ☐ Newfoundland and Labrador
- ☐ New Brunswick
- ☐ Nova Scotia
- ☐ Ontario
- ☐ Quebec
- ☐ Saskatchewan
- ☐ Prince Edward Island

Territories

- ☐ Northwest Territories
- ☐ Nunavut
- ☐ Yukon Territory

Canada Day Teacher Resource Page

BULLETIN BOARD IDEA

- Title
- Colorful Border
- Student Question
- Teacher Example
- Children's Work
- Rubric Score/ Teacher Feedback
- Rubric
- State Standard

Lesson Extensions

- Since Canada Day is celebrated during the summer, students can create journals about their plans for summer vacation. Create a bulletin board using the journals.
- Learn Canada's national anthem.
- Have students conduct a research report about a city, province, or territory in Canada.

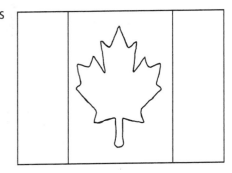

Word Bank

Canada
province
territory
dominion
celebration
festival
patriotic
flag
concert
North America

Children's Literature Ideas

Use for read-alouds, shared reading, silent reading, research, and so on.

Kalman, B. & Walker, N. (1999). *Canada from A to Z.* Crabtree Publishing. ISBN: 0865054118.

Kalman, B. (2001). *Canada the Culture.* Crabtree Publishing. ISBN: 0778797287.

Landau, E. (2000). *Canada.* Scholastic, Inc. ISBN: 0516270214.

Little, C. (2003). *What's It Like to Live in Canada?* School Specialty Children's Publishing. ISBN: 1577688783.

Moore, C. (2002). *The Big Book of Canada: Exploring the Provinces and Territories.* Tundra Publishing. ISBN: 0887764576.

Ulmer, M. (2004). *M Is for Maple: A Canadian Alphabet.* Thompson Gale Publishing. ISBN: 1585362352.

Father's Day

How do you celebrate your father (or father figure) on Father's Day? What is Father's Day, and how did it come to be?

Mrs. John B. Dodd first proposed the idea of a "father's day" in 1909. She thought of the idea while listening to a Mother's Day sermon, and she wanted a special day to honor her father, William Smart. He was a Civil War veteran who was left to raise a newborn and his five other children by himself on a rural farm in eastern Washington state after his wife died in childbirth. As Mrs. Dodd grew up and had a family of her own, she realized the selflessness of her father and the sacrifices he made as a single parent.

She held the first Father's Day in Spokane, Washington, on June 19, 1910. Since her father was born in June, she chose that month for her Father's Day celebration. She had the support of the mayor of her town, Spokane, and the governor of Washington.

The idea was well received, and various other towns and cities began to celebrate fathers, too. In 1924 President Calvin Coolidge even supported plans for a national Father's Day, but it didn't become official until 1966, when President Lyndon Johnson signed a presidential proclamation declaring the third Sunday of June as Father's Day. Later, in 1972, President Richard Nixon signed a law ensuring that the holiday would continue.

Today we honor our fathers and those important men in our lives who serve as role models and mentors. Small gifts and cards are the most popular ways to show our appreciation. So on that third Sunday in June, don't forget to show your appreciation and gratitude to the "father" in your life.

Name: _____   Date: _____

| Dad | Daddy | Uncle | Grandfather | family |
| Father | Papa | Grandpa | care | brother |

Illustrate these four words:

Uncle

Father

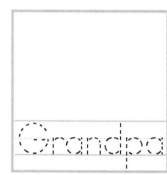
family

Grandpa

What fraction of the ties have polka dots?

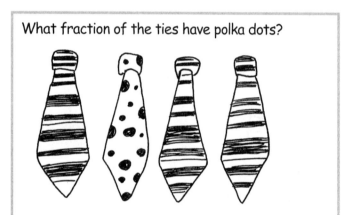

Which one of these items would you most likely give to your dad for Father's Day? Circle it.

WORLD'S GREATEST DAD

Make a list of gifts you could give to your dad for Father's Day.

GIFTS FOR DAD!

Design and draw a tie on Dad for Father's Day. Color the picture when you finish your design.

Name: _____   Date: _____

Illustrate these four words:

Grandfather

family

Papa

Uncle

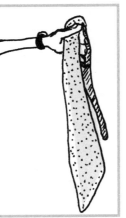

Dad has 85 red ties and 9 green ties. What percent of his ties are green?

Circle the person who would *not* receive a card on Father's Day.

Write a Father's Day poem.

Design a Father's Day card.

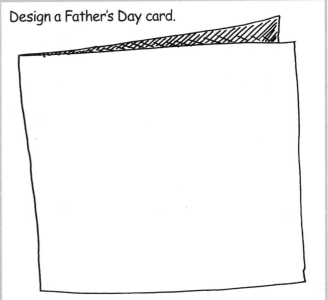

165

Name: _____ Date: _____

How do you celebrate your father or father figure? Draw a picture of you with your father or father figure.

_____

_____

_____

Word Bank Dad Father Daddy Papa Uncle Grandpa Grandfather care family brother

Father's Day Standing Tie Card:

Write about what Father's Day means to you on the tie. Color it, cut it out, and glue the tie to the front of a folded construction-paper card. Decorate your card and write a note inside to the father figure in your life.

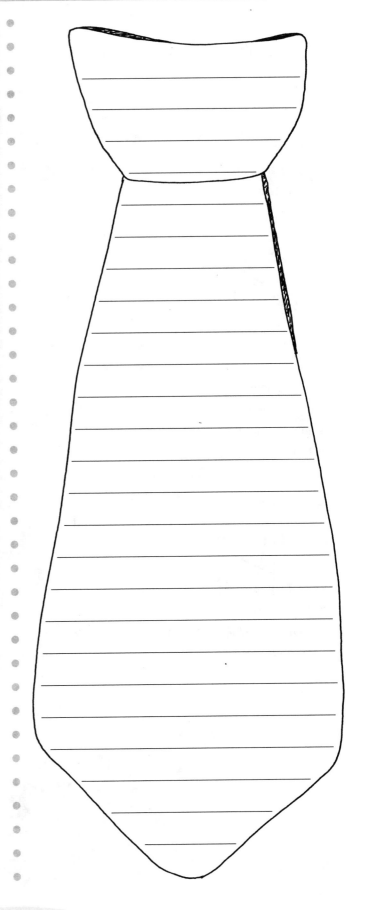

Father's Day Tie Card

Materials

scissors
pencil
crayons
paper
yarn or beads
decorative paper
glue

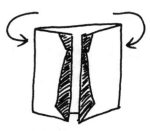

1. Make a photocopy of the template for each of your students. Have them start by cutting out the card.

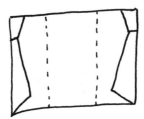

2. Now the card is ready to be folded.

3. Fold the sides backward on the dotted line.

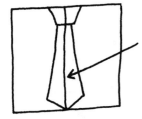

4. Students can color the tie and decorate the cover.

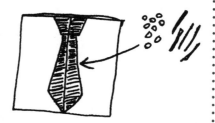

5. For a creative pop, the tie can be decorated with beads, craft paper, or yarn.

6. When finished decorating the outside, glue decorative paper inside for a nice card or poem for Dad.

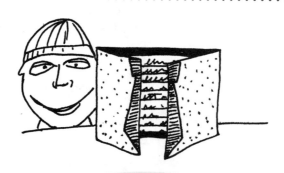

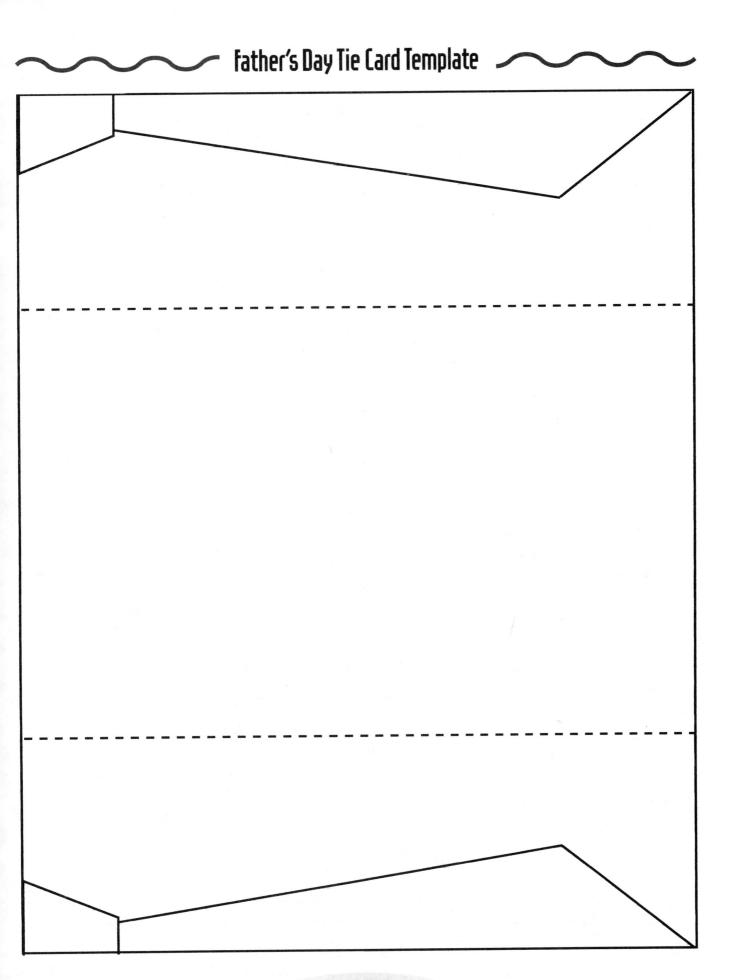

Father's Day Teacher Resource Page

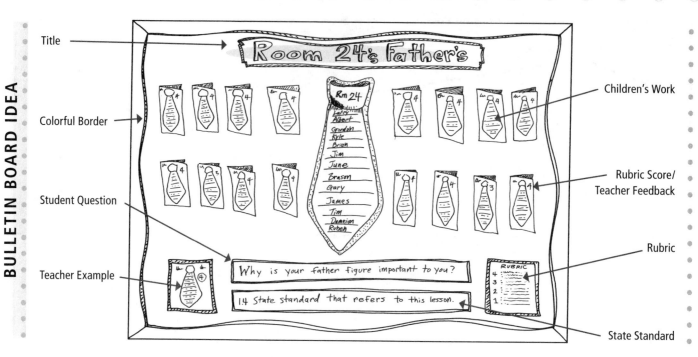

- Title
- Colorful Border
- Student Question
- Teacher Example
- Children's Work
- Rubric Score/ Teacher Feedback
- Rubric
- State Standard

Room 24's Father's

Rm 24
Larry
Albert
Gordon
Kyle
Brian
Jim
June
Brason
Gary
James
Tim
Dameion
Ruben

Why is your father figure important to you?

14 State standard that refers to this lesson.

RUBRIC
4
3
2
1

Lesson Extensions

- Use tie cards to create a Father's Day bulletin board. List the names of the father figures that students have in their lives. (Remember not everyone will have a father figure.)
- Invite fathers or father figures into the class to read, discuss their careers, or volunteer.
- Assign a student and father (or father figure) project related to your curriculum. (Students and fathers have to build or create something as a team.)
- Have students do a report on their father or father figure.

Word Bank

Dad
Father
Daddy
Papa
Uncle
Grandpa
Grandfather
care
family
brother

Children's Literature Ideas

Use for read-alouds, shared reading, silent reading, research, and so on.

Carlisle, B. & Carlisle, B. (2001). *Butterfly Kisses.* Golden Books. ISBN: 0307988724.

Loomis, C. (2004). *The 10 Best Things About My Dad.* Scholastic, Inc. ISBN: 0439577691.

Meddaugh, S. (1993). *Perfect Father's Day.* Houghton Mifflin. ISBN: 0395664160.

Porter-Gaylord, L. (2004). *I Love My Daddy Because . . .* Penguin Books. ISBN: 0525472509.

Steptoe, J. (2001). *In Daddy's Arms I Am Tall: African Americans Celebrating Fathers.* Lee and Low Books, Inc. ISBN: 1584300167.

Independence Day

In Congress July 4, 1776
A Declaration
United States of America

Prior to its independence, the United States was a group of British colonies. The people who lived in the colonies were unhappy about being forced to pay taxes to England without having a say in how the tax money was used. They held a meeting, called the First Continental Congress, in 1774 to find a reasonable solution to their tax situation. The British government sent British troops to the colonies to handle any possible rebellion over taxes, and in April 1775, those troops advanced on Concord, Massachusetts, where weapons were stored for the colonists' rebellion. "The British are coming!" was shouted by Paul Revere as he rode through the night to warn colonists of the impending trouble. The Battle of Concord marked the start of the fight for American independence and was called the "shot heard round the world" because of its worldwide significance.

To try to resolve this conflict, the Second Continental Congress met the next year. These delegates met in Philadelphia and drafted the Declaration of Independence, which broke the colonies' ties to Britain and established their independence. The congress adopted the document on July 4, 1776, which is considered the day American independence was born.

Through the years, thousands of immigrants have come to the United States in search

of a better life known as the "American Dream." The United States is a diverse nation made up of people from various cultural, linguistic, religious, and socioeconomic backgrounds. Many of the early immigrants passed through New York City's harbor when they first arrived in the United States. One of the first things these early immigrants saw when they arrived was the Statue of Liberty. This statue was given to the United States by France in the late 1880s as a symbol of the alliance between the countries during the American Revolution and to signify friendship. She is called "Lady Liberty" and is one of the United States' great icons representing freedom.

July 4 is the day the United States celebrates its birthday. Families celebrate with parades, picnics, and barbecues, traditionally ending with firework displays. It is a time to come together as a community and celebrate the freedom that democracy in the United States gives us. The United States is truly a combination of various cultures and ethnic groups. We have the unique opportunity to learn about other cultures right here. Other languages, religions, and cultural traditions are available to us and make this country what it is. None of this would be possible if we didn't have the freedom and liberties that democracy gives us. July 4 is more than a picnic, parade, or apple pie; it is an opportunity to be thankful for our liberties and to be proud to be Americans.

Name: _____ Date: _____

Illustrate these four words:

There were 5 apple pies at the Fourth of July picnic. Each pie was cut into 8 slices. There were 32 people at the picnic. If each person had a piece of pie, how many extra pieces were left over? _____

Color Lady Liberty.

torch = liberty

July 4, 1776

7 points = 7 continents and seas

broken chains = freedom from tyranny

Finish and color the U.S. flag.

Symbols and Colors of the U.S. Flag

The flag has 13 alternating stripes, 7 red and 6 white. The stripes represent the 13 original colonies. There are 50 stars, each star representing one of the 50 states.

Red represents hardiness and valor.

White represents purity and innocence.

Blue represents vigilance, perseverance, and justice.

Name: _____   Date: _____

Illustrate these four words:

fireworks

stripes

stars

flag

20 pies were brought to the Fourth of July Day picnic. 6 were peach, 10 were apple, and 4 were cherry. Write the fraction and percent each type of pie represented out of the total number brought.

Peach = _____ _____%

Apple = _____ _____%

Cherry = _____ _____%

Learn "The New Colossus," a poem inscribed on a plaque at the base of the Statue of Liberty:

Give me your tired, your poor,
Your huddled masses yearning to breathe free,
The wretched refuse of your teeming shore.
Send these, the homeless, tempest-tossed, to me
I lift my lamp beside the golden door.

—"The New Colossus"
Emma Lazarus

Color and finish the U.S. flag.

Symbols and Colors of the U.S. Flag

The flag has 13 alternating stripes, 7 red and 6 white. The stripes represent the 13 original colonies. There are 50 stars, each star representing one of the 50 states.

Red represents hardiness and valor.

White represents purity and innocence.

Blue represents vigilance, perseverance, and justice.

Name: _____ Date: _____

Write about Independence Day and how it is celebrated. Illustrate.

_____

_____

_____

Word Bank   flag   America   freedom   United States   star   stripe   immigrant   fireworks   liberty   celebration

Name: _____   **Date:** _____

Write about Independence Day and how it is celebrated. Illustrate.

_____

_____

_____

_____

_____

_____

_____

_____

_____

_____

_____

_____

_____

Word Bank   flag   America   freedom   United States   star   stripe   immigrant   fireworks   liberty   celebration

Student Stars

When we celebrate Independence Day, we think of the Stars and Stripes as symbols on our flag. Students can create individual student stars, and the class as a whole can create a classroom flag.

Materials

paper
scissors
crayons
string
tissue paper
hole punch

Create Fourth of July Stars

1. Cut out, color, and decorate.
2. Attach tassels to tips using a hole punch and tissue paper.
3. Hang from a string.

Create a Classroom Flag

1. Students can draw and color their portraits on stars and then cut them out.
2. Attach stars to a large rectangle of butcher paper.
3. Measure and divide by 13. Add 7 red stripes.
4. Write historical facts or liberties we share on the stripes.

U.S. Flag

There are many ways to make a U.S. flag. Try any of these three options.

1. Photocopy the template and have students color it. For stars, tear and glue small torn pieces of white construction paper.
2. Start with plain white paper and glue a blue square down along with 7 red stripes. Use white chalk to draw in the 50 stars.
3. Photocopy the template and glue down torn stripes, blue square, and stars for a more artistic touch.

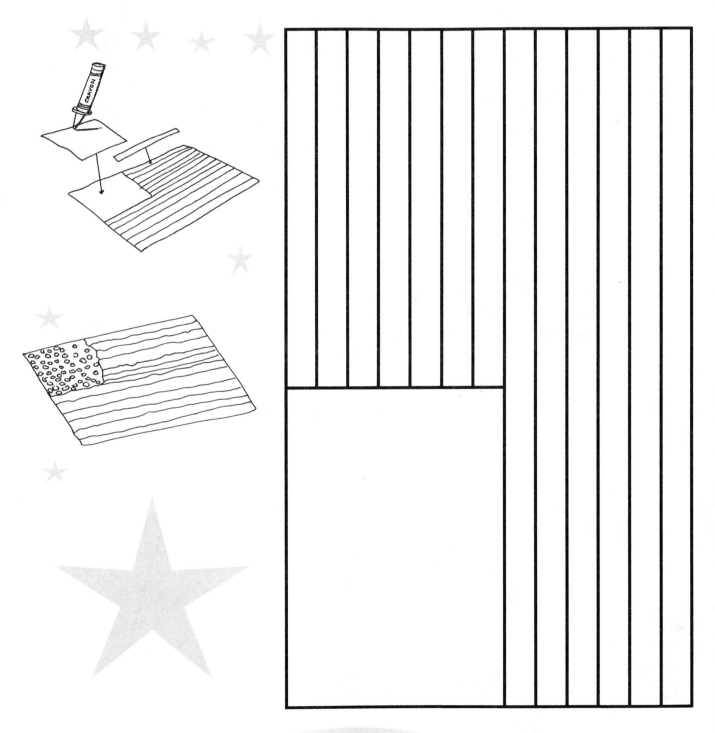

Independence Day Teacher Resource Page

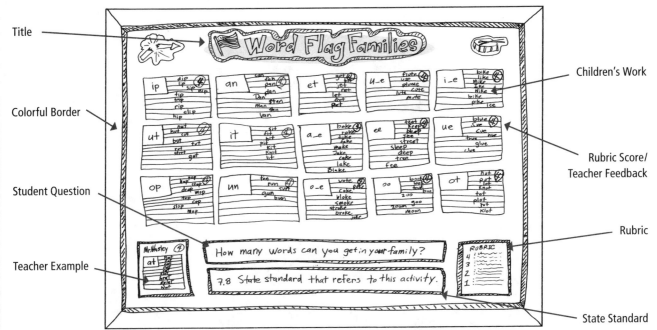

Title

Colorful Border

Student Question

Teacher Example

Children's Work

Rubric Score/
Teacher Feedback

Rubric

State Standard

Lesson Extensions

- Have students create Word Family Flags. Display on a bulletin board.
- Have students develop a time line of how Independence Day came to be. Have them include illustrations at key years.
- Have students write about what freedom means to them.

Word Bank

flag
America
freedom
United States
star
stripe
immigrant
fireworks
liberty
celebration

Children's Literature Ideas

Use for read-alouds, shared reading, silent reading, research, and so on.

Arndt, U. (2001). *Fireworks, Picnics, and Flags: The Story of July Symbols.* Houghton Mifflin. ISBN: 061809654X.

Brenner, S. & Nardo, D. (2003). *Declaration of Independence.* Thomas Gale Publishing. ISBN: 0737710349.

Murray, J. (2005). *Independence Day.* ABDO Publishing, Co. ISBN: 1591975883.

Nelson, R. (2003). *Independence Day.* Lerner Publishing Group. ISBN: 0822512742.

Osborne, M. (2005). *Happy Birthday, America.* Roaring Book Press. ISBN: 1596430516.

Labor Day

How often do we celebrate those who put in many hours each week working to make other people's lives better? Once a year there is a special day dedicated to the hard work people do all year. Labor Day celebrates working people. It was first held on Tuesday, September 5, 1882, in New York City. Union workers wanted to celebrate working people with a parade that showed all the strength of labor organizations. In addition to the parade, there were fun activities for workers and their families.

In 1884, the first Monday in September was selected by the Central Labor Union as the day to honor all workers. Then, in 1894, Congress officially estab-lished Labor Day as a national holiday to be cele-brated on that first Monday. Each year, all Americans honor the dedication, hard work, and remarkable achievements of American workers.

Early in American history, labor groups were formed to protect workers and their rights. Many colonial craftsmen were members of guilds, forerun-ners of unions. With industrialization, labor unions were formed. These unions consisted of workers with jobs in the same industry or trade. Workers found strength in numbers. Labor unions can help protect and improve their members' rights, working conditions, and wages. All of this is done through negotiation and sometimes strikes. A strike is when the workers collectively refuse to work until their contract needs are met. Strikes are usually last resorts in contract negotiations.

One of the United States' most famous laborers was Cesar Chavez. He fought nonviolently for migrant farm laborers and founded the United Farm Workers (UFW), which fought for better wages and safer working conditions. (March 31 is Cesar Chavez Day and is a recognized holiday in some states.)

The United States is not the only country with a celebration for working people. Since the 1880s, Labor Day has also been celebrated on the first Monday in September in Canada. Other countries, including England, use May 1 as a day to honor workers.

Today Labor Day is a special holiday that continues to salute the American worker. For many, Labor Day signals the unofficial end of summer and the start of school. But it is important to remember the true purpose of Labor Day—to celebrate past and present workers who helped build our country and continue to serve as this nation's backbone of strength, leadership, and democratic ideals.

Name: _____   **Date:** _____

Illustrate these four words:

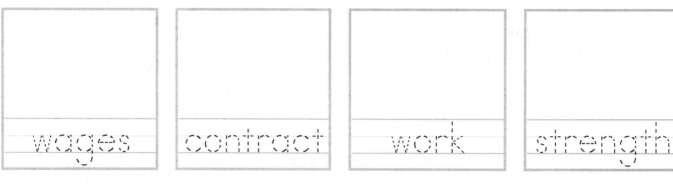

wages   contract   work   strength

In our community, there are many community workers. There are 12 firefighters, 15 police officers, and 20 construction workers. How many community workers are there in all?

Many community workers use tools in their jobs. Circle the tool that would not belong to a construction worker. Color tools they would use.

Tim is a community helper. Choose a job for Tim, and draw his uniform and any tools or materials he may need for his job.

Illustrate how you celebrate Labor Day.

Name: _____   Date: _____

work	strength	organization	strike	migrant
labor	union	guild	contract	wages

Illustrate these four words:

labor	*contract*	*migrant*	*wages*

The top four community jobs in a city are:

   15 firefighters   30 police officers

   40 construction workers   15 teachers

What is the total number of workers?

Write the fraction and percent for each.

Labor Day Trivia

The first Labor Day was on Tuesday, _____.

In _____ Con-gress established Labor Day as a national holiday. Labor Day is celebrated on _____ each year.

Finish drawing Bob the community helper. Include his uniform and any tools or materials he may need for his job.

Illustrate how you celebrate Labor Day.

Name: _____

Date: _____

Write about Labor Day, and illustrate how you observe it.

_____

_____

_____

Word Bank   work   labor   strength   union   organization   guild   strike   contract   migrant   wages

Name: _____ Date: _____

Write about Labor Day and its history.
Illustrate how you observe Labor Day.

_____

_____

_____

_____

_____

_____

_____

_____

_____

_____

_____

_____

Word Bank   work   labor   strength   union   organization   guild   strike   contract   migrant   wages

Community Helpers

There are a variety of community helpers/workers in every neighborhood. They can be doctors, teachers, nurses, construction workers, restaurant employees, bankers, and many others. Take this opportunity to create one you admire from your own community.

Materials

paper
scissors
crayons
tape or glue

Occupation/Job Title: _____

Education/Training Needed: _____

Special Skills Needed: _____

Tools/Instruments Needed: _____

Work Location/Site: _____

How They Serve the Community: _____

1. Create your own community of helpers.

2. Have students select a community helper template or create their own.

3. Have students color, cut out, and glue their helpers so that they stand.

4. Have students research their selected community helpers.

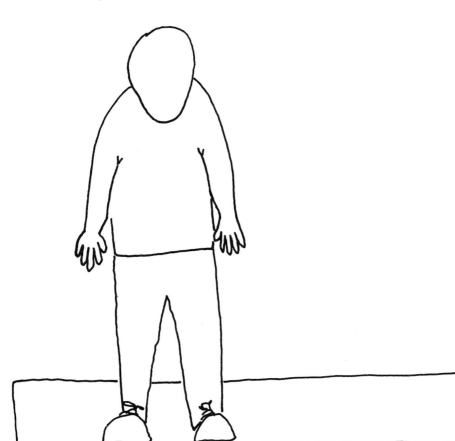

Community Helpers

Community Helpers

GLUE

GLUE

Labor Day Teacher Resource Page

Title

Colorful Border

Student Question

Teacher Example

Children's Work

Rubric Score/
Teacher Feedback

Rubric

State Standard

Labor Day
Community Helpers

Who are the people that help your community?

4.2 State standard that refers to this activity.

RUBRIC
4
3
2
1

Lesson Extensions

- Create a Community Helper bulletin board. Assign a community job to each student. Have them research and write about their jobs. Display reports on the bulletin board.
- Invite a union representative to come in and discuss his or her position and the role and importance of unions today.
- Invite community workers of various unions to come in and discuss their jobs and how their unions help them.

Word Bank

work
labor
strength
union
organization
guild
strike
contract
migrant
wages

ON STRIKE
we need higher wages!

Children's Literature Ideas

Use for read-alouds, shared reading, silent reading, research, and so on.

Ansary, M. (1998). *Labor Day.* Heinemann. ISBN: 157572703X.

Bredeson, C. (2000). *Labor Day.* Scholastic Library Publishing. ISBN: 0516263129.

Hamilton, L. (2004). *Labor Day.* Weigh Publishers, Inc. ISBN: 1590361296.

Schuh, M. & Saunders-Smith, G. (2003). *Labor Day.* Capstone Press. ISBN: 0736816534.

Ramadan

Each year people of the Muslim faith participate in the Fast of Ramadan. Ramadan is the ninth month of the Muslim calendar. The Islamic calendar, like the Gregorian calendar, has 12 months. The Gregorian calendar is based on the sun, and each month has 30 or 31 days, except February. A lunar calendar, the Islamic calendar is based on the moon. Its months have 29 or 30 days, so the celebration of the month of Ramadan lasts 29 or 30 days (depending on the year).

The month of Ramadan is believed to be when the Quran, the Muslim holy text, was sent from heaven as a guide and means of salvation. In approximately A.D. 610 the chosen prophet of Islam, a caravan merchant trader named Muhammad, was on a spiritual retreat in the desert near the city of Mecca in modern-day Saudi Arabia, when Allah (the Muslim word for God) chose him to receive the Quran. He spent the rest of his life dedicated to the Islamic faith and spreading the word of Islam.

During Ramadan, devout Muslims fast from sunrise to sundown each day as ordered by God in the Quran. At night they break their fast with prayer and a meal called Iftar. During this month, they also spend time with family and friends and visit their mosque, their place of worship, to pray and study the Quran.

People who are ill or traveling and need to eat usually break the fast until they can fast for the number of days they missed at another time. Those who are too old to fast pay charity to someone in need every day that they can't fast. Children sometimes participate by fasting for only part of the day. Children can also participate by collecting money for the poor and needy.

Fasting requires strength. It is not easy to go without food or drink for a day. Muslims use this time to build strength and to control their bodies mentally and physically. This strength, in turn, helps them build self-control in all areas of their lives. They pray and depend on God to help them with their fast, which makes them more obedient to God, more blessed, and happier.

Fasting also helps Muslims in life when a difficult choice comes their way. They have the strength to say "no" because of what they learned by fasting. Fasting also helps them understand what it feels like to go hungry. They understand the importance of giving and helping those in need. Fasting is also a chance for the body to rest and use up its extra weight. Lastly, fasting with other Muslims from around the world unifies and strengthens the Muslim community.

This is a very special time devoted to family, self-reflection, and spiritual growth. Muslims worship and think about their lives. It is also a time to strengthen family and community ties.

Finally, Ramadan is also a time to remember those in need and the poor. Charity is very important. Giving time, money, love, respect, dignity, and forgiveness is all part of the month of Ramadan. Muslims believe that this then extends beyond Ramadan and into their attitude and self-control throughout the year.

The most important night during the month is the 27th night of Ramadan. This is a night of power, remembering when the prophet Muhammad received the Quran from God during this month long ago. This night is said to be the night that God determines what will happen in the world during the next year.

At the end of Ramadan, a three-day celebration ends the fasting. It is called *Id-al-Fitr/Eid ul-Fitr*, which translates to "the Feast of Fast Breaking." Muslims exchange gifts and gather together for prayer and feasts. In many cities there are fairs and other large celebrations.

191

Name: _____   Date: _____

Illustrate these four words:

mosque

fast

lunar

charity

During Ramadan, Farah saved coins to give to charity. She saved: 3 pennies   6 nickels
                                                                     1 dime   2 quarters

How much money did she save in all? _____ ¢

Circle the items that you give up during a fast.
What month do Muslims fast from sunup to sundown?

DRINK

Lunar Phases

The Islamic calendar is a lunar calendar, based on the phases of the moon. As the moon orbits the Earth, it moves through eight phases due to its position as well as the positions of the sun and Earth.

We see different portions of the moon through its 29.5-day (month-long) cycle. When more of the moon gets darker each night, it is "waning." When more of the moon gets lighter each night, it is "waxing."

Learn the phases of the moon. Draw and label the phases.

| New Moon | Waxing Crescent | First Quarter | Waxing Gibbous | Full Moon | Waning Gibbous | Last Quarter | Waning Crescent |

○ ○ ○ ○ ○ ○ ○ ○

Name: _____   Date: _____

| Muslim | mosque | charity | Iftar | Muhammad |
| Ramadan | lunar | Islamic | Quran | fast |

Illustrate these four words:

mosque	*charity*	*lunar*	*fast*

During Ramadan, Farah saved coins for charity. She saved:

- 32 pennies
- 13 quarters
- 15 nickels
- 2 dimes

How much money does she have in all? _____

Fill in the Blanks

_____ is the ninth month in the Muslim calendar. The _____ is the holy text given to _____. During Ramadan, Muslims fast from _____ to _____.

Lunar Phases

The Islamic calendar is a lunar calendar, based on the phases of the moon. As the moon orbits the Earth, it moves through eight phases due to its position as well as the positions of the sun and Earth.
We see different portions of the moon through its 29.5-day (month-long) cycle. When more of the moon gets darker each night, it is "waning." When more of the moon gets lighter each night, it is "waxing."
Learn the phases of the moon. Draw and label the phases.

New Moon	Waxing Crescent	First Quarter	Waxing Gibbous	Full Moon	Waning Gibbous	Last Quarter	Waning Crescent

Name: _____

Date: _____

Tell what you have learned about Ramadan, and draw a picture to illustrate.

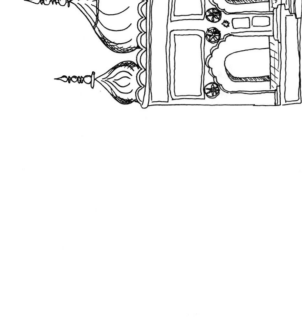

_____

_____

_____

Word Bank   Muslim   Ramadan   mosque   lunar   charity   Islamic   Iftar   Quran   Muhammad   fast

Name: _____ Date: _____

☪ Tell what you know about Ramadan. Illustrate.

_____

_____

_____

_____

_____

_____

_____

_____

_____

_____

_____

_____

_____

Word Bank   Muslim   Ramadan   mosque   lunar   charity   Islamic   Iftar   Quran   Muhammad   fast

Ramadan Fanoos

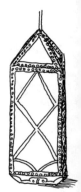

One tradition of Ramadan practiced by some and enjoyed by children is *fanoos*, which means "lanterns." The tradition dates back to Egyptian leader Fatimid Caliphate. Every year on the night before Ramadan, Caliphate would go out to look for the moon, which marked the beginning of Ramadan. The children would go out with their lanterns, fanoos, to light the way for him. The children would sing and welcome Ramadan, each excited to have their own fanoos. Fanoos are made of tin and colorful glass and come in a variety of shapes and sizes. They are lit the nights after fasting is broken to fill the streets with colorful lights.

Materials

· · · · ·

paper
scissors
crayons
hole punch
string or yarn
glue

1. Color and cut out.
2. Fold and glue flap.
3. Punch a hole in the top of each triangle.
4. Secure string or yarn.
5. Display.

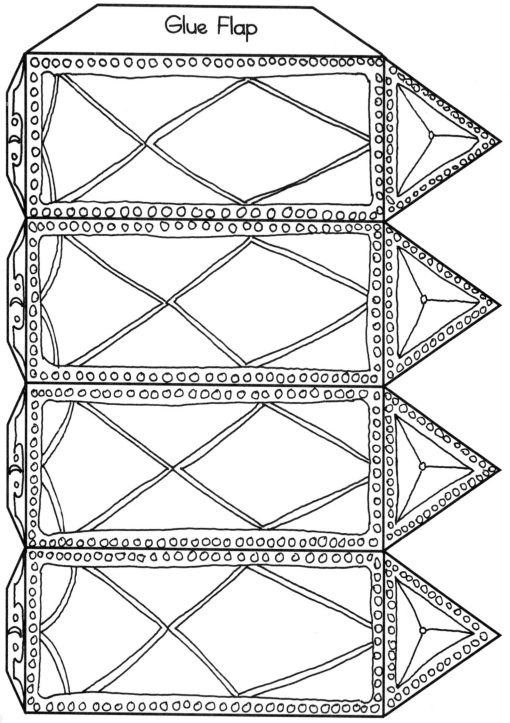

Glue Flap

Ramadan Teacher Resource Page

Title

Colorful Border

Student Question

Teacher Example

Children's Work

Rubric Score/
Teacher Feedback

Rubric

State Standard

How do you plan to celebrate Ramadan

5.9 State standard that refers to this activity.

RUBRIC
4
3
2
1

Lesson Extensions

- Create a bulletin board with the lanterns and journals from the activities.
- Arrange a visit to a local mosque.
- Invite a Muslim parent or community member to speak with your class.
- Bring in samples of traditional Muslim foods for students to try.

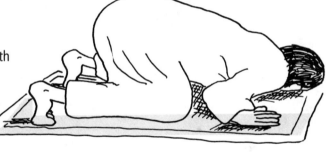

Word Bank

Muslim
Ramadan
mosque
lunar
charity
Islamic
Iftar
Quran
Muhammad
fast

Children's Literature Ideas

Use for read-alouds, shared reading, silent reading, research, and so on.

Douglass, S. (2003). *Ramadan.* Lerner Publishing Group. ISBN: 1575055848.

Heiligman, D. (2006). *Celebrate Ramadan and Eid Al-Fitr with Praying, Fasting, and Charity.* National Geographic Children's Books. ISBN: 0792259262.

Hoyt-Goldsmith, D. (2002). *Celebrating Ramadan.* Holiday House, Inc. ISBN: 082341762X.

Sievert, T. (2006). *Ramadan: Islamic Holy Month.* Capstone Press Sales. ISBN: 0736853928.

Zucker, J. (2004). *Fasting and Dates: A Ramadan and Eid-ul-Fitr Story.* Barron's. ISBN: 0764126717.

Columbus Day

Long ago the world was believed to be flat. Some scholars, however, disagreed, and among them was Christopher Columbus, an Italian navigator. He proposed a voyage to explore the seas, with the purpose of proving that the Earth was round. After being turned down by several countries that refused to pay for his trip, Queen Isabella of Spain agreed to sponsor his voyage. By sailing around the Earth in a more direct route, he was to find for Spain a new trade route to Asia. Not only would he discover a new route, but he would also conquer new lands for Spain. On August 3, 1492, Columbus and 90 men set sail from Spain on three ships: the *Santa María*, with the *Niña* and *Pinta* at her side.

Finally, on October 12, 1492, after a long and hard voyage, the ships landed on the island of Guanahani in the Caribbean Islands. Expecting to see people native to India, Columbus and his men called the people they did see "Indians." But these people were actually the native people of the island called the Taino. Columbus christened the island San Salvador and claimed it for Spain. His ships moved on, and when they landed on what is now Cuba, they thought it was Japan. Columbus made three more trips, four in all, to this new world, not knowing that he had encountered new lands. He died rich and famous but never knew the full implications of what he had found.

Proud Italians began the celebration of Columbus in New York City on October 12, 1866. This celebration grew, and in 1869 the Italians of San Francisco held a similar celebration and called it Columbus Day. Through the years, various states observed Columbus Day, and in 1937, President Franklin Roosevelt issued a public resolution calling for all Americans to celebrate Columbus's life on October 12. In 1971, President Richard Nixon changed the celebration slightly, declaring the federal public holiday would occur each year on the second Monday of October.

There can be controversy when people today say that "America was discovered by Columbus," since Native Americans were indigenous to the land at the time of Columbus's arrival. Therefore, this day is also known as "Indigenous People's Day" in parts of the country.

Name: _____   Date: _____

| Christopher Columbus | ship | island | sail | ocean |
| voyage | native | indigenous | expedition | discover |

Illustrate these four words:

island	ocean	sail	ship

Columbus had three ships on his first voyage. Copy their names.

 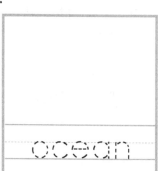 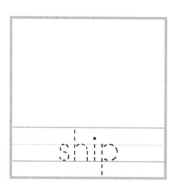

Niña   Santa María   Pinta

4 ships are sailing. 7 more join them.
How many ships are there in all?

_____ ◯ _____ = _____

Illustrate the problem:

Complete the picture of Columbus.

Name: _____ Date: _____

Word Bank				
Christopher Columbus	ship	island	sail	ocean
voyage	native	indigenous	expedition	discover

Illustrate these four words:

island

ocean

sail

ship

Columbus sailed 24 miles to the next island. He returned to the first island and then sailed 30 miles to another island and then returned to the first island. How many miles did he sail altogether?

Parts of a Ship _____

sail   mast   hull

Finish the picture of Columbus.

Name: _____

Date: _____

Finish illustrating Columbus's arrival in the new world. Write about the expedition.

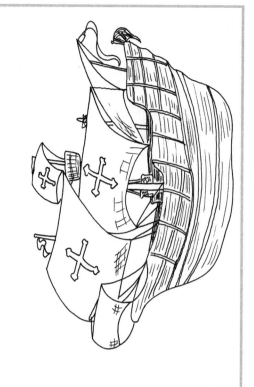

_____

_____

_____

Word Bank Christopher Columbus   voyage   ship   native   island   indigenous   sail   expedition   ocean   discover

Name: _____ Date: _____

Finish illustrating Columbus's arrival in the new world. Write about the expedition.

_____

_____

_____

_____

_____

_____

_____

_____

_____

_____

_____

_____

_____

Word Bank Christopher Columbus voyage ship native island indigenous sail expedition ocean discover

Name: _____

Date: _____

Finish illustrating Columbus's arrival in the new world. Write about the expedition. Then cut out and insert the ship.

Columbus's Ship

Color Columbus's ship. Cut out the ship and mount it on a Popsicle stick. Use the story paper on the next pages. Fold it and cut on the dotted line. Slide the ship into the slit, and move the ship as the student's story about the voyage is read.

Materials

paper
scissors
crayons
tape
Popsicle stick

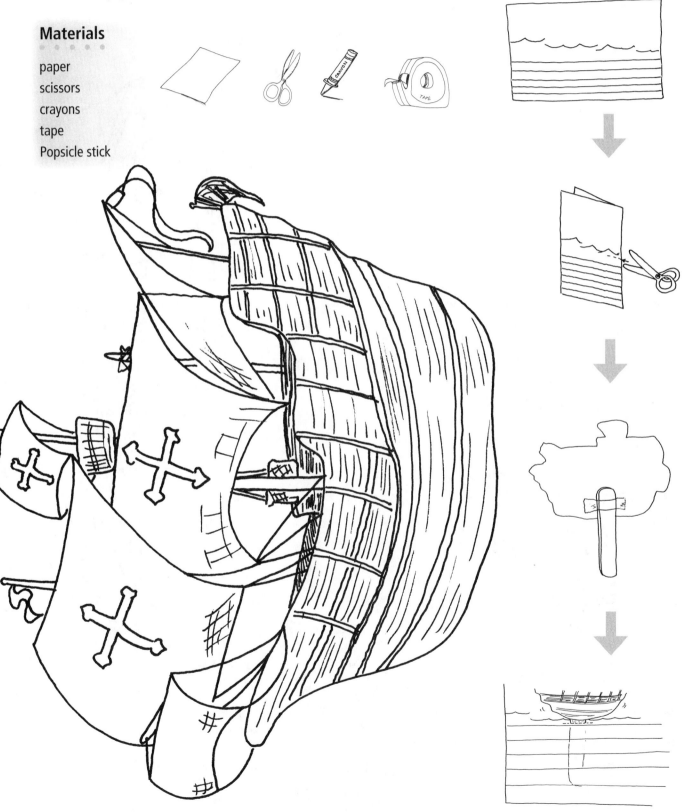

Columbus's Ship

Color the ship's hull, and then cut out and attach the story journal sail. Create a mast, other sails, and even flags to decorate your ship.

Materials

paper
scissors
crayons
tape

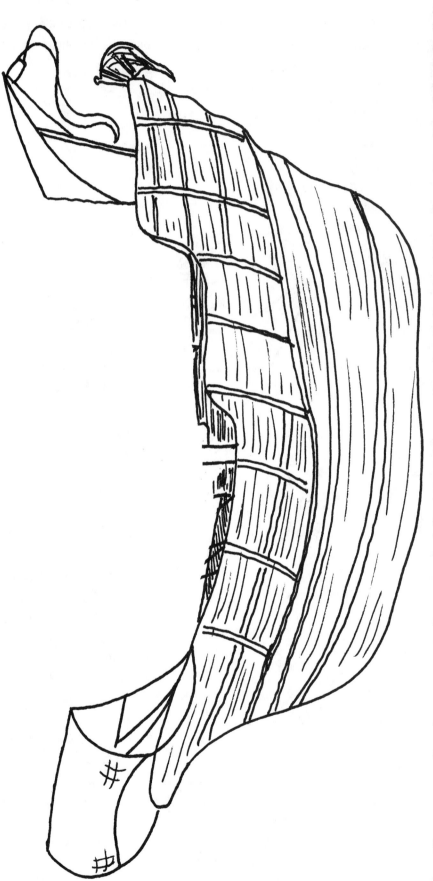

Columbus's Ship Journal Page

Write about what you've learned about Columbus's journey.

Columbus Day Teacher Resource Page

Title

Colorful Border

Student Question

Teacher Example

Children's Work

Rubric Score/
Teacher Feedback

Rubric

State Standard

What do you know about Columbus Day?

1.9 State standard that refers to this activity.

RUBRIC
4
3
2
1

Lesson Extensions

- Create a ship bulletin board using the activity template. Have students write what they've learned about Columbus's journey on the sail. Create the ships and then display on the bulletin board.
- Have students develop a historical time line with the most crucial events of Columbus's voyages.
- Have students research and write reports about the lives of the Native Americans, specifically the Taino Indians, indigenous to the lands Columbus arrived at.

Word Bank

Christopher Columbus
voyage
ship
native
island
indigenous
sail
expedition
ocean
discover

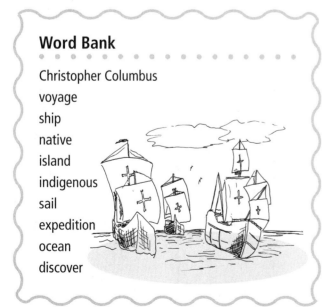

Children's Literature Ideas

Use for read-alouds, shared reading, silent reading, research, and so on.

Dorris, M. (1999). *Morning Girl.* Hyperion. ISBN: 07861358X.

Fritz, J. (1998). *Around the World in a Hundred Years: From Henry the Navigator to Magellan.* Penguin Putnam. ISBN: 0698116380.

Larkin, T. (2003). *Christopher Columbus.* Rosen Publishing Group, Inc. ISBN: 0823955540.

Murray, J. (2005). *Columbus Day.* ABDO Publishing, Co. ISBN: 159197875.

Yolen, J. (1996). *Encounter.* Harcourt. ISBN: 015201389X.

Halloween

Each year on October 31, children dress up in their favorite costumes, go door-to-door, and collect candy from neighbors and community members by saying, "Trick or Treat." Seeing the creative costumes and trying to guess who might be behind each mask adds to the fun. To add to the playful atmosphere, lit jack-o'-lanterns (pumpkins with carved out faces) with their glowing eyes can be seen on many people's front porches. But how did it all begin?

The name *Halloween* dates back to the eighth century and All Saints' Day, a religious holiday celebrating saints each year on November 1. All Saints' Day was once called "All Hallows' Day," and the day before was called "All Hallows' Eve," which became "All Hallow E'en" and, eventually, "Halloween."

The actual traditions of Halloween date back even further to the Celtic New Year, the night of October 31. Celts were the ancestors of the Irish, Welsh, and Scottish. It is believed that October 31 was the night ghosts actually walked the Earth and interacted with the living. The Celts would bake lots of food and even dress up like the souls of the dead. The food was carried to the edge of the town so that the ghosts would leave before midnight of the new year.

Eventually Christianity spread throughout Ireland. At the same time a new calendar was adopted

and October 31 was no longer the New Year. But the tradition of Halloween did not die; it continued as a celebration mostly for children. In the 1840s, Irish immigrants brought this tradition to the United States.

In 18th-century America, Halloween was a night of mischief and pranks, often referred to as "Mischief Night." By the 1930s children started to go door-to-door and ask for a treat, a much nicer alternative to the pranks of "Mischief Night." However, if no treat was offered, the children could potentially play a trick on that house. This is where we get the Halloween expression "Trick or Treat."

The Halloween tradition has continued and grown into a very commercialized holiday. Costumes are now mostly store-bought and range from cartoon characters to scary goblins. Many adults even like to dress up for the day. There are costume parties and dances, school parades, and large street festivals each year. So remember to be ready with your treats on October 31 to avoid any tricks.

210

Name: _____   Date: _____

Illustrate these four words:

pumpkin

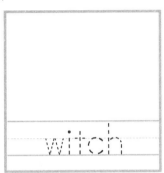
witch

candy

costume

Illustrate and write the number sentence.
4 pieces of candy are in the pumpkin. 8 more pieces are put in the pumpkin. How many candies are there in all?

Which one of these will help a pumpkin grow? Circle it.

Add details to each picture to make it fit the title. Color.

jack-o'-lantern

pumpkin

Connect the dots to make a Halloween surprise. Color.

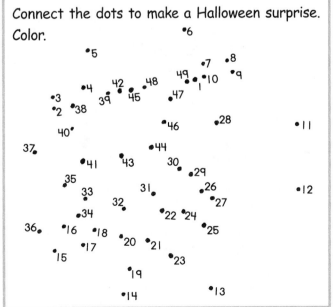

Name: _____   Date: _____

Word Bank	October	costume	trick or treat	jack-o'-lantern	witch
	masks	candy	scary	ghost	pumpkin

Illustrate these four words:

mask   *trick or treat*   *ghost*   *costume*

There are 386 candies in the bowl.
Kashala gives away 132 candies at 7:00 P.M.
At 8:00 P.M. she gives away 135 more.
How many candies are left in the bowl?

Research and name the parts of the skeleton.

_____   _____

_____   _____

Draw the meal you would prepare for ghosts. After you draw your meal, list the food items and how much of each item you would serve.

Item	Amount

Draw three children trick-or-treating in their costumes.

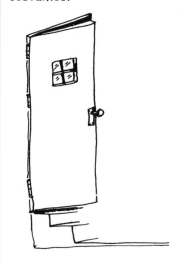

Name: _____

Date: _____

Halloween Writing: Write about how you plan to celebrate Halloween.

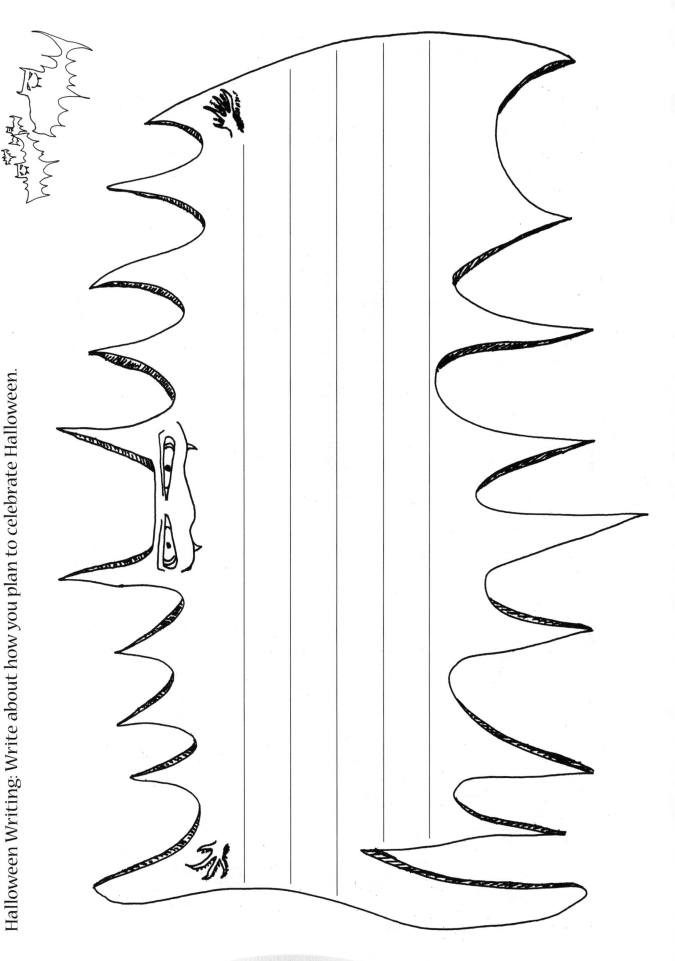

Halloween Journal: Write about how you plan to celebrate Halloween.

Halloween Pumpkin Patch

Follow the directions and design a pumpkin patch to use with story problems.

1. Cut out pumpkins and glue.

2. Cut and glue vines.

3. Create story problems to solve for sums, differences, fractional parts, or percents.

Stuffed Candy Skull

Students can make great Halloween skulls that can be filled with treats.

Materials

skull template
scissors
crayons
stapler

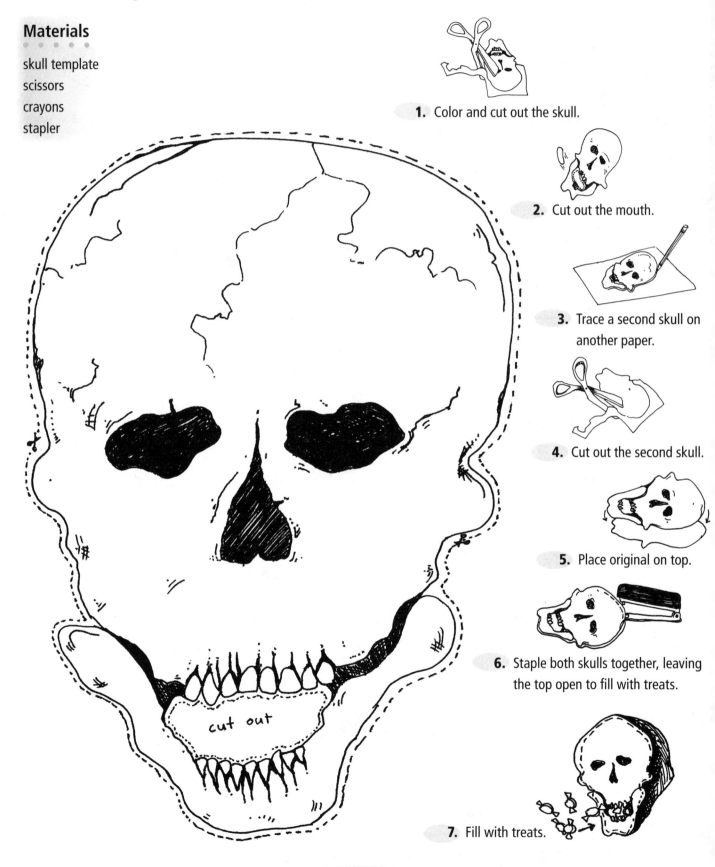

1. Color and cut out the skull.

2. Cut out the mouth.

3. Trace a second skull on another paper.

4. Cut out the second skull.

5. Place original on top.

6. Staple both skulls together, leaving the top open to fill with treats.

7. Fill with treats.

cut out

Halloween Teacher Resource Page

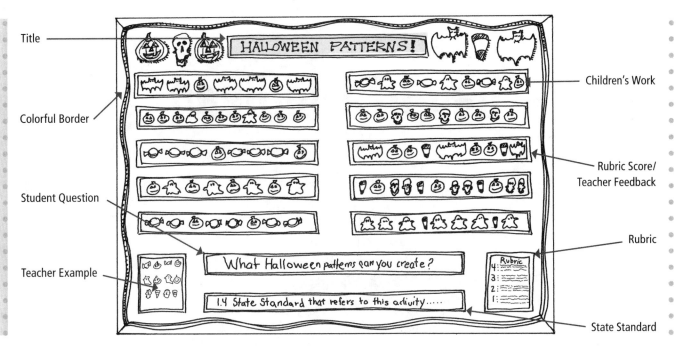

Title

Colorful Border

Student Question

Teacher Example

Children's Work

Rubric Score/
Teacher Feedback

Rubric

State Standard

HALLOWEEN PATTERNS!

What Halloween patterns can you create?

1.4 State Standard that refers to this activity.....

Rubric
4:
3:
2:
1:

Lesson Extensions

- Create a Halloween Pattern bulletin board.
- Predict the sizes of pumpkins. Then, measure pumpkins with strips of paper and compare strip lengths.
- Have the class gather all of their pumpkin patch cutouts together on one desk, and practice counting them in different groups (2's, 5's, and 10's). Extend this into other counting games!
- Play Halloween Concentration. Illustrate each of the words in the Word Bank on cards (picture on one side and word on the other), making two of each card. Put all cards face-down and play by matching two of the same. You can add extra words to make the game more difficult.

Word Bank

October
masks
costume
candy
trick or treat
scary
jack-o'-lantern
ghost
witch
pumpkin

Children's Literature Ideas

Use for read-alouds, shared reading, silent reading, research, and so on.

Crum, S. (2001). *Who Took My Harry Toe?* Albert Whitman Publishers. ISBN: 0807559725.

Kline, S. (2002). *Horrible Harry at Halloween.* Penguin Putnam. ISBN: 0141306750.

Rylant, M. (2003). *Moonlight: The Halloween Cat.* HarperCollins. ISBN: 0060297115.

Seinfeld, J. (2002). *Halloween.* Little, Brown and Co. ISBN: 0316706256.

Ziefert, H. (2001). *On Halloween Night.* Penguin Putnam. ISBN: 0140568204.

Day of the Dead

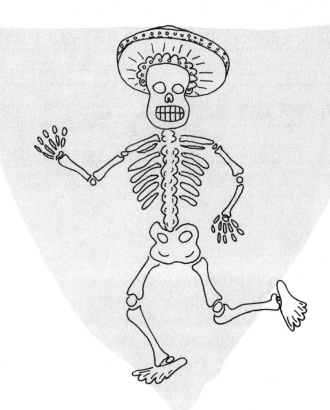

On the Day of the Dead (*Día de los Muertos*), people in Mexico and many parts of the world remember and honor their dead relatives. The festival typically takes place on November 1 (All Saints' Day) and November 2 (All Souls' Day). In Mexico it is a national holiday that has ancient Aztec and Mesoamerican roots. The Day of the Dead is also celebrated in other Latin American countries and even in the Philippines. Celebrations have spread with those who have immigrated to other countries as well. In the United States, many Mexican-American communities continue the tradition.

For this holiday, families decorate their homes with special home altars featuring playful imagery of human skeletons and leave offerings, or *ofrendas*, of food and favorite items of the deceased to welcome the spirits of the dead back into their homes. They also visit the gravesites of close relatives who have died. At the cemetery, they clean and decorate the grave with flowers and have a picnic. A prominent flower used in the celebration is the orange marigold, the "flower of the dead," or "*flor de muerto.*" These family picnics become community celebrations as other families are also picnicking at the gravesites of their deceased loved ones.

It is believed that the souls of the dead return and are around their living relatives. Picnics are sure to include traditional, colorfully decorated sugar

skulls, *calaveras de azucar*, that bear the name of the deceased or recipient when given as a gift. The skulls are a common symbol of this celebration. Bread of the dead, *pan de muerto*, is also a tradition. This is a sweet egg bread often formed into different shapes, from animals to skulls. Guatemalans celebrate the day by visiting the cemetery and flying homemade paper kites, other traditions also imitated in the United States.

Although this holiday focuses on the dead, it is not a sad day; instead it is a joyous celebration of the lives of those who have died. It celebrates the continuation of life, the next chapter in our existence. What a wonderful way to keep the memories of loved ones alive and well in our hearts. So on November 1 and November 2, take time to celebrate any loved ones that have passed away by visiting their gravesites, sharing stories about them with others who knew them, or just spending time with your memories of them.

Word Bank	celebration	spirit	skeleton	altar	marigold
	dead	honor	offering	grave	skull

Illustrate these four words:

skull

skeleton

marigold

grave

3 skeletons are dancing. 8 more join them. How many skeletons are there in all?

_____ ◯ _____ = _____

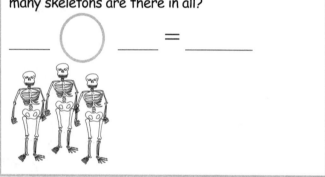

Color the matching skulls the same color.

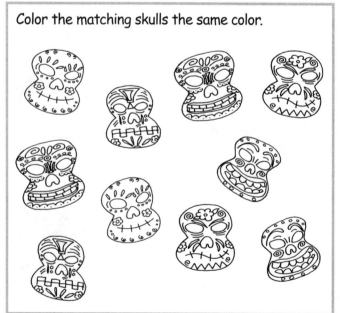

Parts of a Skeleton

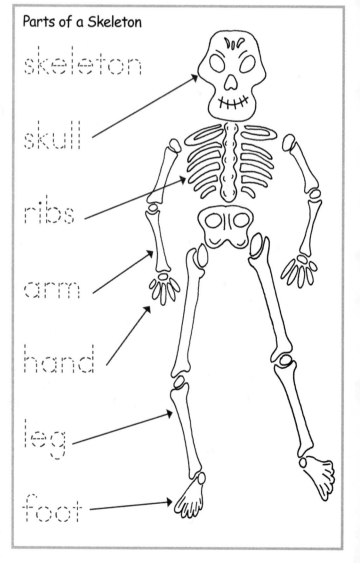

skeleton

skull

ribs

arm

hand

leg

foot

Name: _____   Date: _____

Illustrate these four words:

grave

marigold

skull

skeleton

Parts of a Skeleton

skull ribs pelvis spine
clavicle humerus elbow
radius ulna wrist femur
patella tibia fibula
phalanges (×2)

Label:

_____
_____
_____
_____
_____
_____
_____
_____
_____
_____
_____
_____

To celebrate the Day of the Dead, a class of 30 students made sugar candy skulls. They made five dozen of the happy skull and three dozen of the sad skull. Each student ate one skull. How many skulls remained? If the remaining skulls were divided equally among the students, how many skulls would each student take home? How many would be left over?

Day of the Dead

On the Day of the Dead, the people of _____

celebrate and honor

_____. They

decorate with special

_____. They

leave offerings of_____

for the _____.

They even visit _____.

They celebrate from _____

to _____.

Name: _____

Date: _____

Finish illustrating the celebration. Write about
what you would include in your celebration.

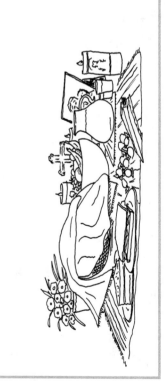

_____

_____

_____

_____

Word Bank   celebration   dead   spirit   honor   skeleton   offering   altar   grave   marigold   skull

Name: _____   Date: _____

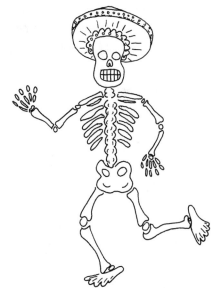

Finish illustrating the celebration. Write about how you would celebrate the life of a deceased relative.

_____

_____

_____

_____

_____

_____

_____

_____

_____

_____

_____

_____

_____

_____

Word Bank   celebration   dead   spirit   honor   skeleton   offering   altar   grave   marigold   skull

Build a Skeleton

Skeletons, or *calaveras* in Spanish, have always been an important symbol of Day of the Dead celebrations. Oftentimes they are brightly colored, dressed, and depicted in real-life scenarios.

Create your own *calaveras* by cutting out the skeleton parts and assembling them into a skeleton. After skeletons have been glued onto sheets of paper, they can be decorated.

Materials

paper
crayons
scissors
glue

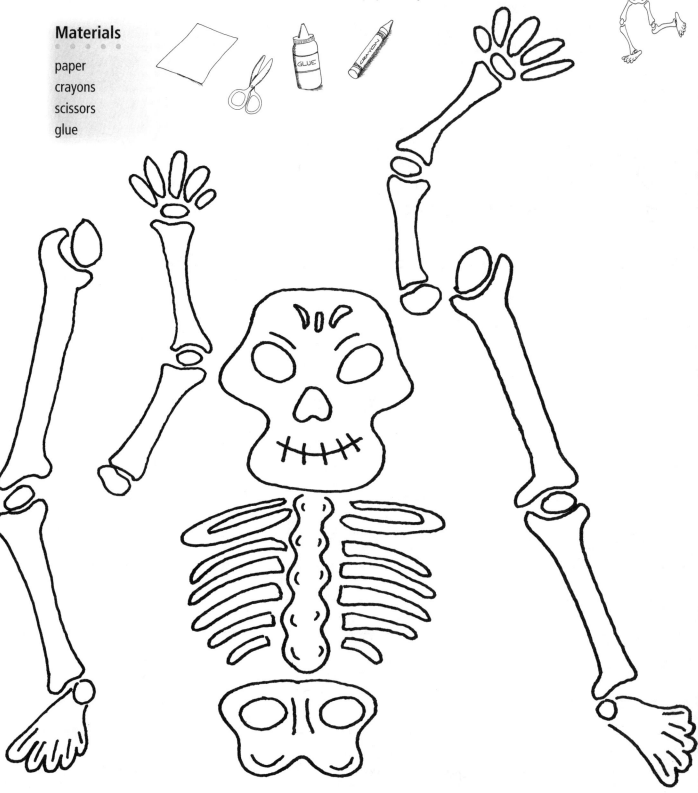

224

Matching Skulls

Color and cut out the cards. Play a memory matching game.

Skull Mask

Materials

paper
crayons
scissors
glue
paper plate
string

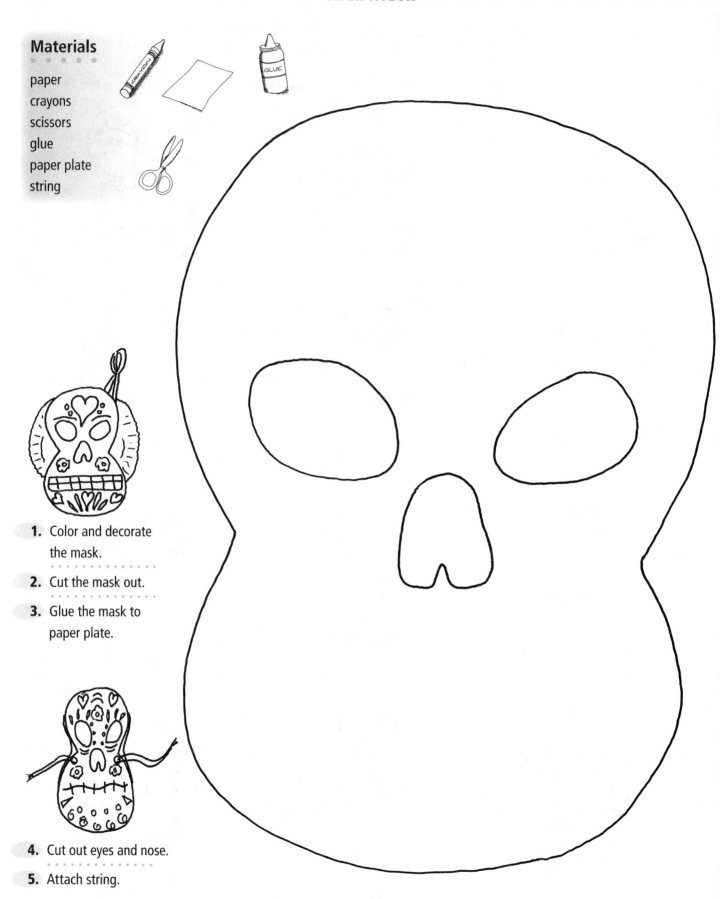

1. Color and decorate the mask.
2. Cut the mask out.
3. Glue the mask to paper plate.
4. Cut out eyes and nose.
5. Attach string.

226
© The McGraw-Hill Companies, Inc.

Day of the Dead Teacher Resource Page

Title

Colorful Border

Student Question

Teacher Example

Children's Work

Rubric Score/
Teacher Feedback

Rubric

State Standard

(bulletin board labels) Day of the Dead — Dia De Los Muertos

How do you celebrate Day of the Dead?

2.9 State standard that refers to this activity.

RUBRIC
4
3
2
1

Mr. Erby
Day of the
Dead

Lesson Extensions

- Create skull masks and display on a bulletin board.
- Arrange a field trip to a cemetery. Most cemeteries will take your students on a guided tour, describing the architecture, ways to acknowledge the deceased, and types of rock and materials used to build the mausoleums and other structures on the cemetery property.
- Have students write a letter about what they cherish about a deceased family member or friend.

Word Bank

celebration
dead
spirit
honor
skeleton
offering
altar
grave
marigold
skull

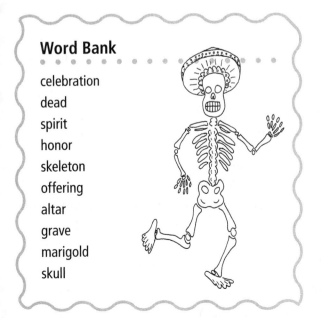

Children's Literature Ideas

Use for read-alouds, shared reading, silent reading, research, and so on.

Coll, I. (2003). *El Día de muertos.* Lectorum Publications, Inc. ISBN: 1930332440.

Johnston, T. (2000). *Day of the Dead.* Harcourt. ISBN: 0152024468.

Keep, R. (2004). *Clatter Bash!: A Day of the Dead Celebration.* Peachtree Publishing. ISBN: 1561453226.

Lowery, L. (2003). *Day of the Dead.* Lerner Publishing. ISBN: 087614914X.

San Vicente, L. & Byrd, B. (2002). *Festival of the Bones/El festival de las Calaveras.* Cinco Puntos Press. ISBN: 0938317679.

Election Day

In America, turning 18 years old brings a very special privilege—the right to vote in elections. In the United States, as long as you are a U.S. citizen 18 years or older, you automatically have the right to vote in local, state, and national elections. You can vote for the mayor, governor, senators, congressmen, or President.

We vote all the time when a group of people make a decision or a choice. In school, students may select monitors for the classroom, vote on a game to be played, or even choose a Student of the Week. In addition, schools usually have elections for student council representatives. All of these activities include voting. Basically, voting includes a choice and people's participation in reaching a decision about that choice.

In addition to choosing leaders, adults vote on local, state, and national levels to decide many issues, including how tax money should be spent and what new laws are needed to protect us. For example, voters may decide where a new park should be built, how much money will be spent to build it, and what equipment will be used.

Today a major problem with voting is the lack of people voting, or low voter turnout. Most elections are lucky if even half of the voters turn out. By not participating, people give up their right to make choices. They have no say in what gets done and who will lead them. Everyone who can vote should vote! It's not very effective to complain about decisions being made if you have not put your voting right into practice.

The right to choose leaders through voting is the basis for a democracy. In the United States, there are major groups that have similar beliefs and opinions about how the country should be run. These groups, called parties, select candidates for elections. The Democrats and the Republicans are examples of political parties in the United States.

When a leader needs to be chosen or something needs to be decided, the options are put on a ballot, the paper that lists all of the choices. A ballot is secretly marked by each voter, and then the ballots are counted to see who or what wins. This process is called an election, and the people listed on the ballot are candidates. When decisions to be made are included on a ballot, such as whether to build a new park or road, they are called propositions. Before the actual election, candidates make flyers and posters, give speeches, and make appearances to let the people know their plan if elected. All these activities are called a campaign. During campaigns candidates talk about the issues and may even debate each other. A powerful tool used in elections is a poll, or sample survey, of what voters think about the issues. On election day, voters vote on their ballots for whom or what they want.

In the United States the official day for national elections is the first Tuesday after the first Monday in November. Local and state elections may happen on other days throughout the year. On Election Day, people report to their polling place, such as a school, church, or public place, where a voting station has been set up and vote. All votes are by secret ballot so no one has to worry about what others might think about his or her choices.

Ballots seem to have originated in ancient Athens and started out as tokens or small balls that were placed in a ballot box. These balls were then counted to decide the winner. Paper ballots date back to Rome, 139 B.C.E., and were first used in the United States in 1629 for a church election. A mechanical lever voting booth was introduced in New York in 1892. Today, many polling places use a punch card or a marked card system that is fed into a computer to count the votes. In recent years, computerized voting machines with touch screens have also become commonplace.

Voting is not only possibly the greatest right one can have but also an exciting process that allows people to have a voice in their community. Every vote counts and adds up to major decisions that everyone should have a say in. Encourage students in your classroom to read about the issues in their community and vote when election day rolls around. You may even want to spend a few weeks

© The McGraw-Hill Companies, Inc.

Democrat

Republican

going through the steps that take place in a real election. Students can pretend to be one of the candidates while others can take on persuading students to vote for certain positions. Students can hold mock debates and prepare posters and flyers. On election day students can hold a mock election and then compare their decision with that of the real one.

U.S. History of Voting

Voting is a right, and it took years to eventually give everyone this right. *Suffrage* is a noun that means "the right to vote." It is the act of voting. Many fought long and hard for suffrage. Today all age-appropriate U.S. citizens, men and women, enjoy this right. A few important dates stand out in the history of voting.

- In 1776 the Declaration of Independence was adopted, giving the right to vote to free white men who owned property.
- In 1870 African American men were given the right to vote in the Fifteenth Amendment.
- In 1920 the Nineteenth Amendment gave women the right to vote.
- In 1947 Native Americans were given the right to vote.
- In 1971 the voting age was lowered from 21 to 18 years.

| democracy | party | opposition | polling | proposition |
| vote | debate | ballot | election | suffrage |

Illustrate these four words:

| ballot | election | debate | vote |

The school elections were held. Ben received 75 votes, and Kristen received 25 votes. Who won the election? How many students voted? What fraction of the votes did each candidate receive?

Winner: _____

Total votes: _____

Ben's fraction of votes: _____

Kristen's fraction of votes: _____

Who got to vote first? List the order that people earned voting rights.

| Women | African Americans | Men | Native Americans |
| _____ | _____ | _____ | _____ |

Draw a possible location for a polling place.

Create a ballot. If your class held an election whom would you elect?

_____ Room _____ Ballot _____

Please select only one candidate for each office. Mark with a check mark.

President

☐ _____   ☐ _____

Vice President

☐ _____   ☐ _____

Secretary

☐ _____   ☐ _____

Treasurer

☐ _____   ☐ _____

Word Bank	democracy	party	opposition	polling	proposition
	vote	debate	ballot	election	suffrage

Illustrate these four words:

debate *ballot* *election* *vote*

Three candidates ran for school president. Candidate A received 30 percent of the votes, candidate B received 45 percent of the votes, and candidate C received 25 percent of the vote. How many votes did each candidate receive if the total number of votes was 200? Who won the election?

Candidate A _____ votes

Candidate B _____ votes

Candidate C _____ votes

Create a campaign poster for an election.

U.S. Voting Time Line

Complete this time line by filling in the year with the significant event of that year.

1776 _____

_____

_____

1870 _____

_____

_____

1920 _____

_____

_____

1947 _____

_____

_____

1971 _____

_____

_____

233

Name: _____

Date: _____

Write about what happens on Election Day. Draw a picture
of something that was voted on in your community.

_____

_____

_____

Word Bank democracy vote party debate opposition ballot polling election proposition suffrage

Name: _____   Date: _____

Write about the democratic process of voting. Illustrate an example of a change made in your community based on the results of an election.

_____

_____

_____

_____

_____

_____

_____

_____

_____

_____

_____

_____

_____

Word Bank   democracy vote party debate opposition ballot polling election proposition suffrage

Election Ballot

1. Cut out the ballot.
2. Cut out and fold the ballot sleeve.
3. Fill in the candidates, the school name, and type of election (classroom officers, school council, etc.).
4. Vote!

☆ **Official Election Ballot** ☆

School Name

Check the box next to selected candidate.
Please vote for only one candidate per office.

Office/Job	Candidate	Vote
		☐
		☐
		☐
		☐
		☐
		☐
		☐
		☐
		☐
		☐
		☐

☆ Election Ballot Sleeve ☆

School Name

Election

Election Day Teacher Resource Page

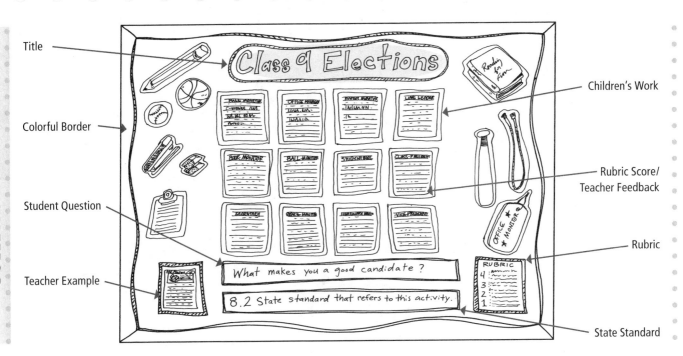

Title — Class 9 Elections

Children's Work

Colorful Border

Rubric Score/ Teacher Feedback

Student Question

Rubric

Teacher Example

What makes you a good candidate?

8.2 State standard that refers to this activity.

RUBRIC

State Standard

Lesson Extensions

- Develop 3–5 classroom propositions, and then have the children vote on them using premade ballots.
- Come up with 2–4 classroom concerns and solutions, and then have students vote on them using a premade ballot.

Word Bank

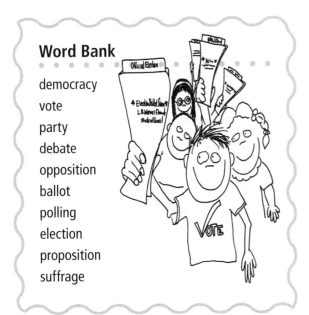

democracy
vote
party
debate
opposition
ballot
polling
election
proposition
suffrage

Children's Literature Ideas

Use for read-alouds, shared reading, silent reading, research, and so on.

Battle-Lavert, G. (2004). *Papa's Mark.* Holiday House, Inc. ISBN: 082341650X.

Bausum, A. (2004). *With Courage and Cloth: Winning the Fight for a Woman's Right to Vote.* National Geographic Society. ISBN: 0792276477.

Christelow, E. (2004). *Vote!* Houghton Mifflin. ISBN: 0618486062.

McNamara, M. (2004). *Election Day.* Simon and Schuster. ISBN: 0689864256.

Nobleman, M. (2004). *Election Day.* Compass Point Books. ISBN: 0756506441.

Veterans Day

Our freedoms, laws, and justice system have been defended throughout history by those who have served in the U.S. armed forces. Many have made tremendous sacrifices and even given their lives for our country. We have rights and privileges that other people in other nations do not have because of these sacrifices. We should never take our rights and freedoms for granted, nor should we forget the past. Remembering those who sacrificed, fought, and even died for us is very important. The United States honors its military veterans with a special day, Veterans Day. This day is set aside to honor veterans—men and women—who have served in the armed forces.

After World War I ended, Veterans Day began as a celebration of the peace. Initially it was called Armistice Day in honor of the truce that finally ended that war, signed on November 11, 1918. In 1938, Armistice Day became an official U.S. federal holiday, to be celebrated on November 11 of each year. In 1954, the holiday was renamed Veterans Day and became an official holiday honoring all U.S. veterans. It continues to be observed on November 11.

Other countries also honor their veterans on this day. The holiday is observed in the United Kingdom, Australia, and Canada as Remembrance Day. In South Africa and Malta, it is celebrated as Poppy Day, named after a field flower that grew in the battlefields of World War I. Britain recently also established a Veterans Day to honor its veterans on June 27.

Remember that this is not just another day off from work or school. It's a day worth recognizing, and one that should be honored by giving thanks to the soldiers who have defended our rights.

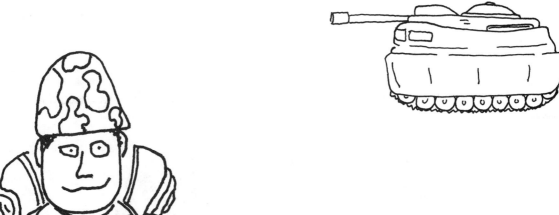

Name: Date:

Illustrate these four words:

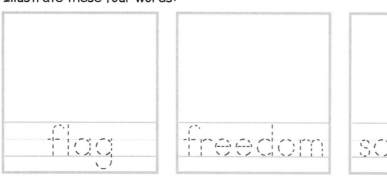

| flag | freedom | sacrifice | medal |

5 veterans marched in a parade. 6 more veterans joined them. How many veterans marched in all?

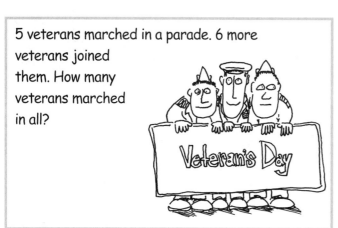

Cross out those who would *not* be veterans.

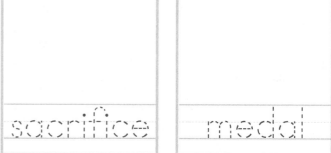

Finish Kenny's flag.

Draw a picture of what you would thank a veteran for.

Word Bank				
defend	medal	sacrifice	U.S. Navy	U.S. Marines
freedom	veteran	armed forces	U.S. Army	flag

Illustrate these four words:

flag

medal

freedom

sacrifice

50 veterans marched in a parade. 10 veterans were under 25 years old; 20 were women; and 5 were older than 70 years old. Write the fraction and percent that represents each group.

< 25 years old

women

> 70 years old

Circle which one a veteran would be awarded. Write one possible reason why.

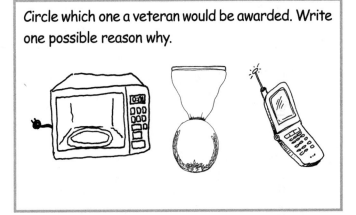

Finish drawing the boy at the parade.

Write three things that you would thank a veteran for.

1. _____

_____

2. _____

_____

3. _____

_____

Name: _____

Date: _____

Write about the significance of Veterans Day, and illustrate a military person in uniform.

_____

_____

_____

Word Bank   defend   freedom   medal   veteran   sacrifice   armed forces   U.S. Navy   U.S. Army   U.S.

Name: _____   Date: _____

· ·

Write about the significance of Veterans Day, and illustrate a military person in uniform.

_____

_____

_____

_____

_____

_____

_____

_____

_____

_____

_____

_____

_____

Word Bank   defend   freedom   medal   veteran   sacrifice   armed forces   U.S. Navy   U.S. Army   U.S. Marines   flag

Veterans Day Peace Dove

Materials

dove template
scissors
string

1. Color the U.S. flag that is draped between the dove halves.
2. Cut out the dove halves and flag in one piece.
3. Fold the paper in half so the dove halves line up.
4. Fold the wings partway down to create a flying dove.
5. Attach dove halves with glue and add string (optional).

244

Medal of Honor

Color the ribbon with the colors and symbols of the flag. The medal may identify a war, battle, or deed of service.

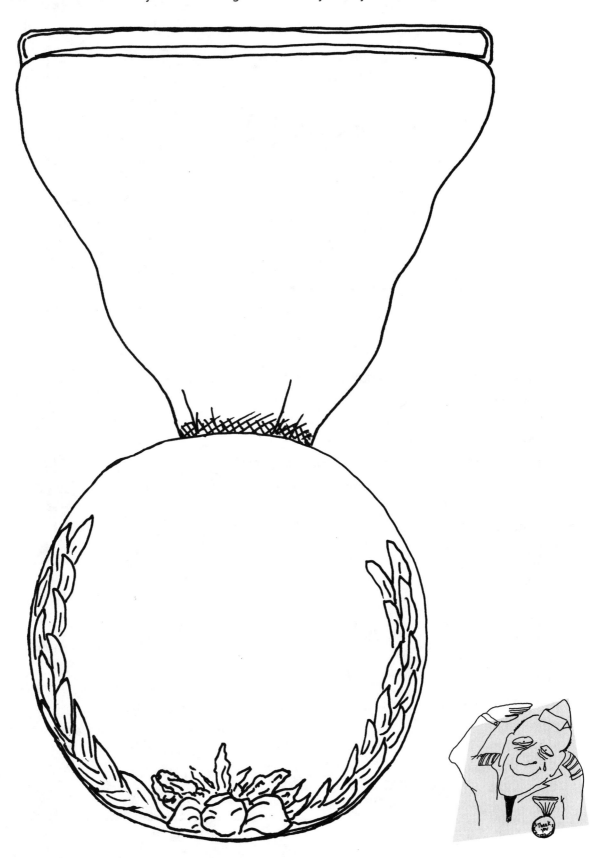

Veterans Day Teacher Resource Page

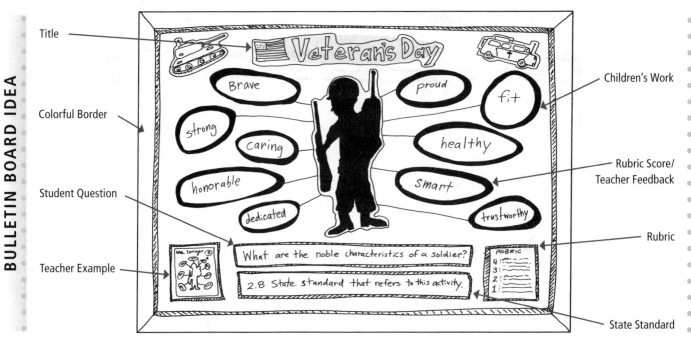

- Title
- Colorful Border
- Student Question
- Teacher Example
- Children's Work
- Rubric Score/ Teacher Feedback
- Rubric
- State Standard

Brave proud fit strong caring healthy honorable smart dedicated trustworthy

What are the noble characteristics of a soldier?

2.8 State standard that refers to this activity.

RUBRIC
4
3
2
1

Lesson Extensions

- Create soldier organizer maps to describe a soldier and display maps on a bulletin board.
- Invite a veteran to class to talk with students about his or her service in the armed forces.
- Have students write a letter to someone in the military, thanking that person for his or her bravery so that everyone can continue to enjoy our freedoms in the United States.
- As a class, prepare 1–5 care packages to be sent to troops.

Word Bank

defend
freedom
medal
veteran
sacrifice
armed forces
U.S. Navy
U.S. Army
U.S. Marines
flag

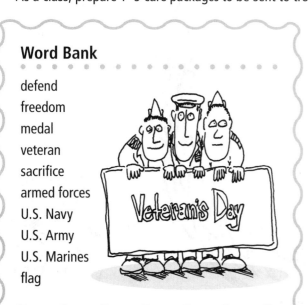

Children's Literature Ideas

Use for read-alouds, shared reading, silent reading, research, and so on.

Crew, G. (2004). *Memorial.* Simply Read Books. ISBN: 1894965086.

Henry, H. (2003). *Pepper's Purple Heart.* Cubbie Blue Publishing. ISBN: 0970634102.

Jorgenson, N. (2003). *In Flanders Field.* Simply Read Books. ISBN: 1894965019.

Landau, E. (2002). *Veterans Day: Remembering Our War Heroes.* Enslow Publishers, Inc. ISBN: 0766017753.

Sorenson, L. (1994). *Veterans Day.* Rourke Publishing. ISBN: 1571030700.

Thanksgiving Day

Both the United States and Canada celebrate their own versions of Thanksgiving Day. In the United States, the celebration takes place on the fourth Thursday in November; in Canada, it is held on the second Monday in October.

On Thanksgiving in the United States, a large feast is prepared, and friends and family gather together to give thanks for the blessings they have. Parades are held in major cities, football games are played, and the winter holiday season customarily starts the day after, with the biggest shopping day of the year. So how did this tradition begin?

The first Thanksgiving was a feast in 1621 that included the Pilgrims of Plymouth Colony and the Wampanoag Indians. Sailing across the Atlantic Ocean from England aboard the *Mayflower*, the Pilgrims had landed at Plymouth Rock on December 11, 1620, in what is now Massachusetts. That first winter was harsh and devastating. Many of the Pilgrims died, unable to survive in the new land. Those who did live needed help, and the Wampanoag Indians, particularly an English-speaking tribe member named Squanto, were helpful in teaching the Pilgrims how to survive. Squanto taught them everything from using fish as a fertilizer for crops to building stronger homes. He also translated and helped build relations between the two groups. The Pilgrims' first fall harvest was successful, and together the Pilgrims

and Wampanoag shared a feast of corn, squash, wild fowl, and much more. This gathering was more of a harvest feast, which was a common practice for both the Pilgrims and the Wampanoag at that time. But due to the tremendous conditions that were overcome that first year, we think of it as the first Thanksgiving. Unlike our annual celebration today, this first feast was not repeated until more than a decade later.

Native Americans actually celebrated "thanksgiving" festivals even before Europeans ever arrived in America. The Wampanoag, for instance, traditionally held several thanksgiving festivals and harvest feasts. Other accounts have been recorded of Spanish, French, and British colonists holding thanksgiving services before and after the famous Pilgrims' celebration in 1621. Most of these early thanksgivings weren't feasts but were more religious in nature, with an emphasis on thanking God.

Although several U.S. Presidents supported a national day of thanksgiving, it was Sarah Josepha Hale, a magazine editor, who worked tirelessly for it. Her 40-year campaign of writing editorials and letters in support of a national thanksgiving day finally paid off in 1863 when President Abraham Lincoln declared Thanksgiving a national holiday.

In Canada, Thanksgiving was declared a national holiday by the Canadian Parliament in 1879, but originally the day had a different meaning entirely. Although it is also a celebration founded by Europeans traveling to the New World, it actually began as a day to celebrate the recovery of the Prince of Wales (later King Edward VII) from a serious illness. The holiday's meaning has changed through the years, and now it is very similar to that in the United States—a day to come together with family to celebrate one's many blessings.

The symbol of Thanksgiving in the United States is a turkey, a term Pilgrims originally used for any wild fowl. Turkey is now the centerpiece of a traditional Thanksgiving feast. Today, family members and friends continue to gather together to enjoy a bountiful feast and to reflect on the many blessings they are thankful for. In addition, churches, individuals, and various groups often gather donated food to deliver to families in need so that they too will have a holiday feast to share with their family and friends.

Name: _____   Date: _____

Word Bank

thankful	Pilgrim	corn	colony	celebration
harvest	Native American	turkey	feast	cornucopia

Illustrate these four words:

turkey

Pilgrim

feast

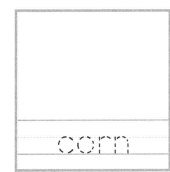

corn

3 turkeys are sitting on the fence. 5 more turkeys join them. How many turkeys are there in all? Write the number sentence to solve the problem and illustrate.

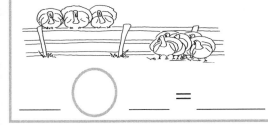

_____ ◯ _____ = _____

Which one of these did the Pilgrims use to prepare their food? Circle it.

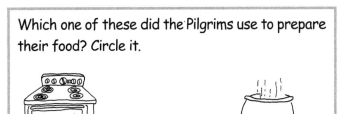

Fill the cornucopia with Thanksgiving food. Color.

Label the parts of a turkey. Complete the drawing.

beak

eyes

feathers

waddle

wings

feet

Word Bank

thankful	Pilgrim	corn	colony	celebration
harvest	Native American	turkey	feast	cornucopia

Illustrate these four words:

turkey	*feast*	*harvest*	*cornucopia*

Illustrate and write the number sentence.
There are 8 turkeys. How many wings, feet, and beaks are there in all?

_____ ◯ _____ = _____ wings

_____ ◯ _____ = _____ feet

_____ ◯ _____ = _____ beaks

_____

Finish illustrating the turkey.

Thanksgiving Facts _____

The first Thanksgiving was celebrated in _____. The _____ Indians attended. Thanksgiving was declared a national holiday in _____ by President _____.

Label the parts of a turkey. Complete the drawing.

beak

eyes

feathers

waddle

wings

feet

Name: _____

Date: _____

Finish illustrating the Thanksgiving celebration. Write about what you would include in your Thanksgiving celebration.

_____

_____

_____

Word Bank   thankful   harvest   Pilgrim   Native American   corn   turkey   colony   feast   celebration   cornucopia

Name: _____   Date: _____

Finish illustrating the Thanksgiving celebration. Write about a Thanksgiving celebration.

_____

_____

_____

_____

_____

_____

_____

_____

_____

_____

_____

_____

_____

_____

Word Bank   thankful   harvest   pilgrim   Native American   corn   turkey   colony   feast   celebration   cornucopia

Build a Turkey

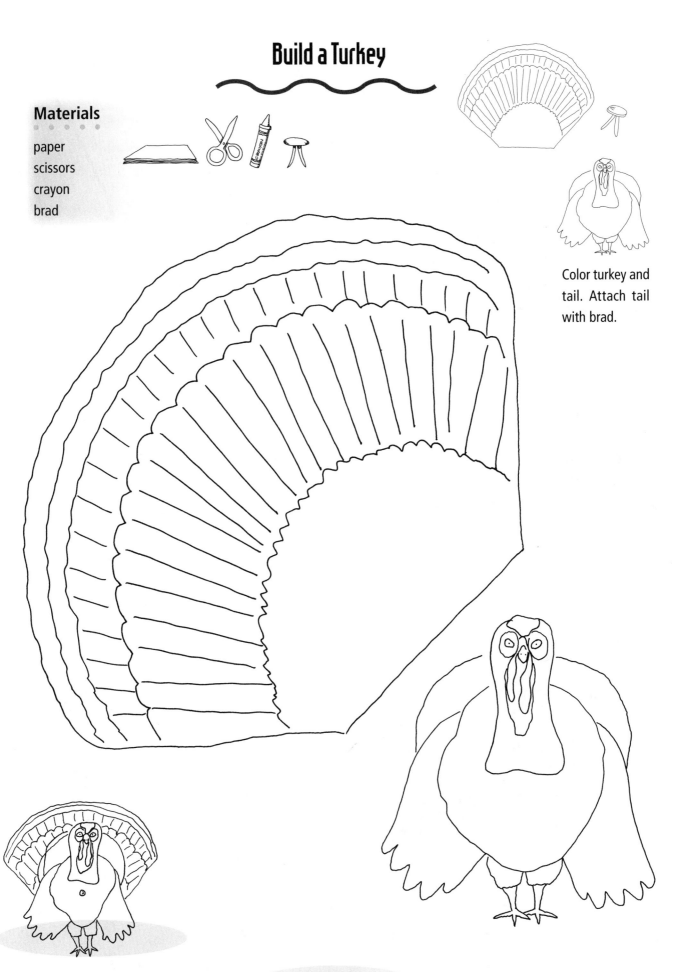

Materials

paper
scissors
crayon
brad

Color turkey and tail. Attach tail with brad.

Turkey Stationery

- Write a poem.

- Write about what you are thankful for.

- Write a note to thank someone.

- Write a Thanksgiving story.

Gratitude Turkey

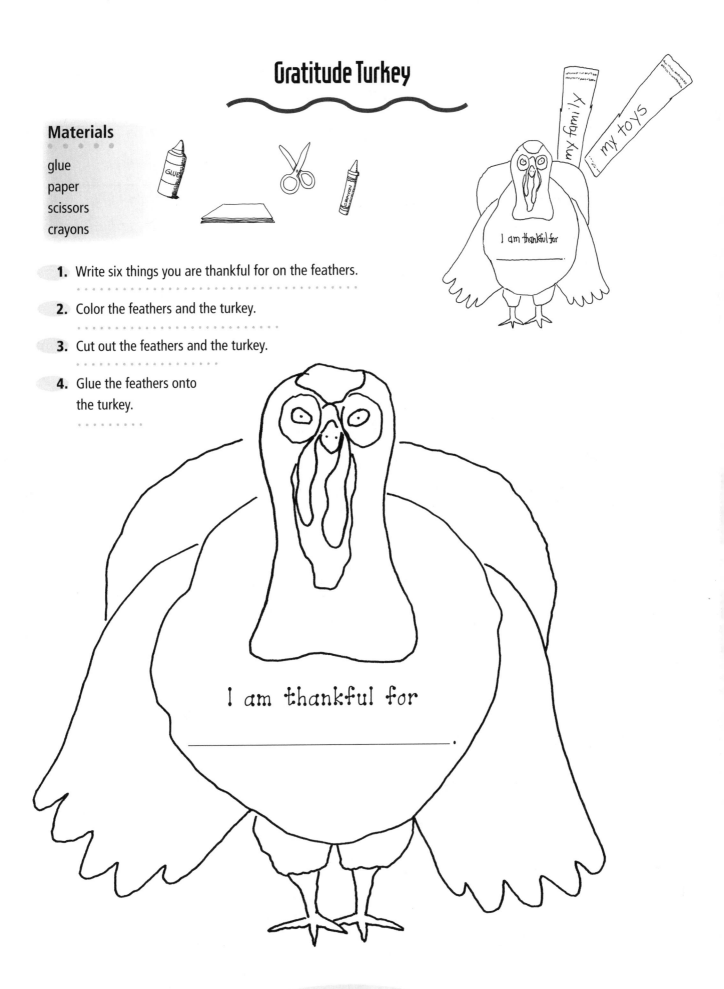

Materials

glue
paper
scissors
crayons

1. Write six things you are thankful for on the feathers.

2. Color the feathers and the turkey.

3. Cut out the feathers and the turkey.

4. Glue the feathers onto the turkey.

my family

my toys

I am thankful for

I am thankful for

Gratitude Turkey Feathers

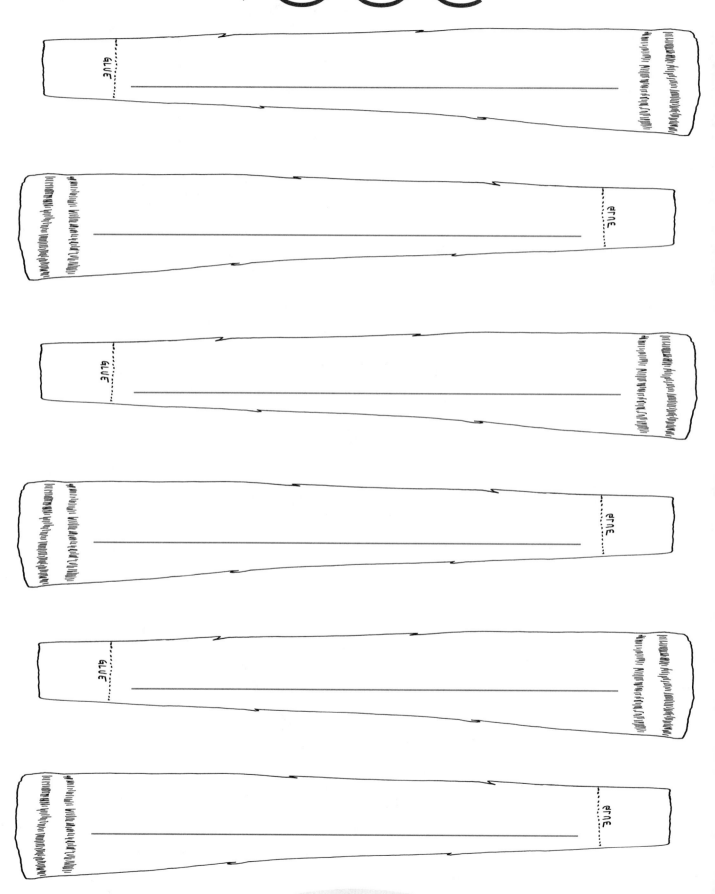

Thanksgiving Day Teacher Resource Page

BULLETIN BOARD IDEA

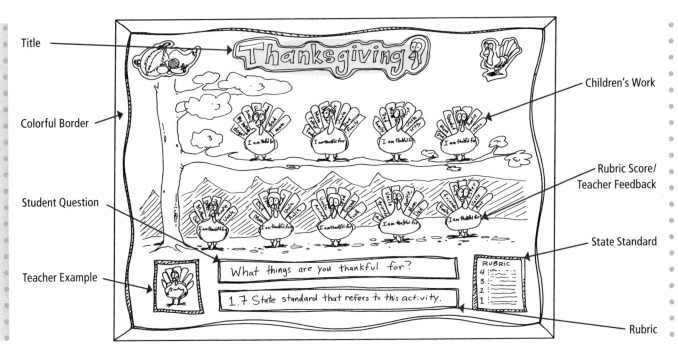

Title

Colorful Border

Student Question

Teacher Example

Children's Work

Rubric Score/
Teacher Feedback

State Standard

Rubric

What things are you thankful for?

1.7 State standard that refers to this activity.

Lesson Extensions

- Create Thankful Turkeys. Have students write about what they are thankful for.
- Have students write a letter to their parents or guardians, a teacher, grandparents, or a friend thanking them for important times together, for taking care of them, or for whatever students are thankful for in their lives.
- Have a Thanksgiving Feast in the classroom. Each student brings a dish to share.

Word Bank

thankful
harvest
Pilgrim
Native American
corn
turkey
colony
feast
celebration
cornucopia

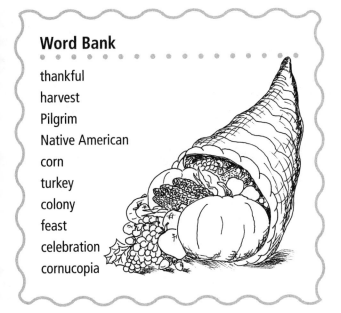

Children's Literature Ideas

Use for read-alouds, shared reading, silent reading, research, and so on.

Bunting, E. (1990). *How Many Days to America?* Houghton Mifflin. ISBN: 0395547776.

Cowley, J. (1998). *Gracias, the Thanksgiving Turkey.* Scholastic, Inc. ISBN: 0590469770.

Kamma, A. (2001). *If You Were at the First Thanksgiving.* Scholastic, Inc. ISBN: 0439105668.

O'Neill Grace, C. (2004). *1621: A New Look at Thanksgiving.* National Geographic Society. ISBN: 0792261399.

Pomeranc, M. (1998). *The Can-do Thanksgiving.* Albert Whitman Publishers. ISBN: 0807510548.

Hanukkah

Hanukkah is a holy eight-day festival in the Jewish tradition. The exact dates can vary as it is always celebrated on the 25th day of the Kislev, the third month in the Jewish calendar. This means Hanukkah generally falls in either late November or December on the Gregorian calendar.

The history of Hanukkah can be traced back more than 2,300 years to Judea, a country where many Jewish people lived under Syrian-Greek rule. King Antiochus did not like the Jewish religion and ordered all the Jewish people to give up their religion and customs. He also ordered them to worship Greek gods and idols. Temples, Jewish places of worship, were taken over or destroyed.

This was a very difficult time for the Jewish people. However, some refused to worship other gods and give up their religion and customs. One man who refused was Judah Maccabee. He and his four brothers banded together with others to form an army. This army fought for the Jewish people, their customs, and their religion. They called themselves the Maccabees, which means "the Hammers," and fought the Syrian-Greeks for about three years, finally defeating them. The victory was considered a miracle, as the 3,000 Maccabees were vastly outnumbered by the 20,000-member Syrian-Greek army.

Having won back their land and freedom, the Jewish people were excited and immediately began to restore their temple in Jerusalem. After removing all of the Greek symbols and idols and cleaning the temple thoroughly, they wanted to rededicate the temple to God. In Hebrew, *Hanukkah* means "rededication." They needed blessed oil to light the temple lamps and especially the menorah, which was sacred and needed to be lit at all times. Oil was difficult to find, but finally, a small amount was located. It was only enough to burn the lamps and menorah for one night. But to their surprise, the oil burned for eight nights, just enough time to make more oil.

Hanukkah is celebrated to remember those who fought for their Jewish faith and for the miracle of the eight days that the oil lasted. It is known as the "Festival of Lights" for the eight days of oil. A menorah is a candelabrum that holds nine candles. Eight candles, representing each night that the oil burned in the lamps of the temple in Jerusalem, are arranged around a central ninth candle, which is slightly higher than the others. Each night of Hanukkah a blessing is given and a candle is lit from the center candle, called the *shamash*. This custom continues for eight days until the final night when all the candles burn brightly.

During Hanukkah children may play the dreidel game. This game, too, has historical significance. Long ago when King Antiochus banned Jewish worship, those who met in secrecy to study the Torah, the Jewish book of worship, would quickly play dreidel if caught. A dreidel is a four-sided top that is spun. It has four letters from the Hebrew alphabet, one on each side. These letters, *nun*, *gimel*, *hei*, and *shun*, stand for the saying "a great miracle happened there." To play dreidel each player places a coin, candy, or marker of some type into the center of a circle and takes turns spinning the dreidel. The Hebrew letter on each side represents how much of the candy the spinner gets to keep or lose at his or her turn. The words can be loosely translated to mean "no win" (*nun*), "take half" (*hey*), "take all" (*gimel*), or "put in another coin" (*shin*).

The celebration of Hanukkah includes many traditional foods that are fried or baked with oil, symbolic of the oil that lasted eight days. Fried potato pancakes, or *latkes*, are an example of a food served. Children traditionally were given coins/money by older relatives for their knowledge of the story of Hanukkah. Today this money, or *gelt*, is often replaced by gifts given during the eight nights of festivities.

Name: _____   **Date:** _____

Word Bank

Hanukkah	Hebrew	lamp	dreidel	gelt
Jewish	temple	menorah	latke	oil

Illustrate these four words:

lamp	dreidel	menorah	latke

Shoshana, Issac, and Eli played dreidel. Ariel watched. Each started with 8 candies. Shoshana won! How many candies did she win in all?

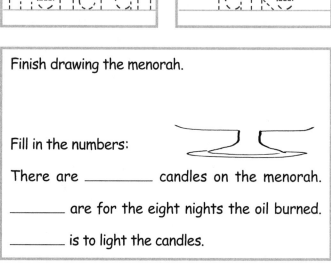

Finish drawing the menorah.

Fill in the numbers:

There are _____ candles on the menorah.

_____ are for the eight nights the oil burned.

_____ is to light the candles.

The dreidel has four Hebrew letters, one on each side. Color the letters and trace their names. Learn what each means when you roll it in dreidel.

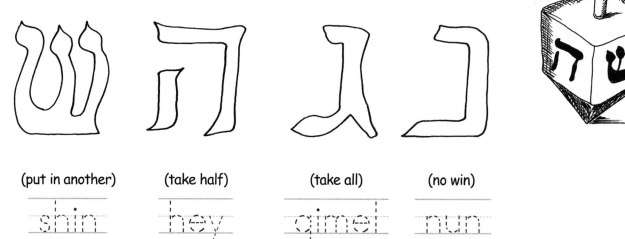

(put in another)	(take half)	(take all)	(no win)
shin	hey	gimel	nun

260

Name: _____   **Date:** _____

Word Bank

| Hanukkah | Hebrew | lamp | dreidel | gelt |
| Jewish | temple | menorah | latke | oil |

Illustrate these four words:

menorah	*dreidel*	*temple*	*lamp*

Shoshana, Issac, and Eli were playing dreidel and then stopped for latkes. Ariel watched. There were 40 candies in all. At the break Shoshana had 20 pieces, Issac had 15, and Eli had 5. What fraction, decimal, and percent of candies did each person have?

Shoshana = _____ _____ _____

Issac = _____ _____ _____

Eli = _____ _____ _____

Hanukkah Trivia
_____

Fill in the blanks: _____ was the king who ordered the Jewish people to give up their religion. _____ fought the king with his brothers and an army. The small amount of oil burned for _____ days. Hanukkah is known as the Festival of _____.

The dreidel has 4 Hebrew letters. Color the letters, and learn their name and what they mean when rolled.

(put in another)	(take half)	(take all)	(nothing)
shin	hey	gimel	nun

Fill in the blanks. Finish drawing the menorah.

There are _____ candles in all on the menorah.

The candles represent _____.

Name: _____

Date: _____

Explain what Hanukkah is and how it is celebrated.
Illustrate.

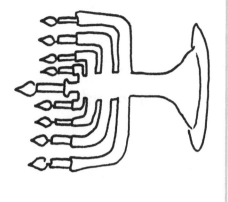

_____

_____

_____

_____

Word Bank   Hanukkah   Jewish   Hebrew   temple   lamp   menorah   dreidel   latke   gelt   oil

Name: _____   Date: _____

Write about the history of Hanukkah and how it is celebrated today.
Illustrate.

_____

_____

_____

_____

_____

_____

_____

_____

_____

_____

_____

_____

_____

Word Bank   Hanukkah   Jewish   Hebrew   temple   lamp   menorah   dreidel   latke   gelt   oil

Menorah

Hanukkah means "rededication." This is when you start over or renew your efforts. Use this menorah to write eight things, one on each candle, that you want to work harder on or renew your energy with. Use the center candle, the *shamash* or the attendant, for your name. You are like the *shamash* in your life—you light all the areas of your life, from reading to sports. Have fun rededicating yourself to these things in your life. Then draw or attach a tissue paper flame to each candle to celebrate your rededication.

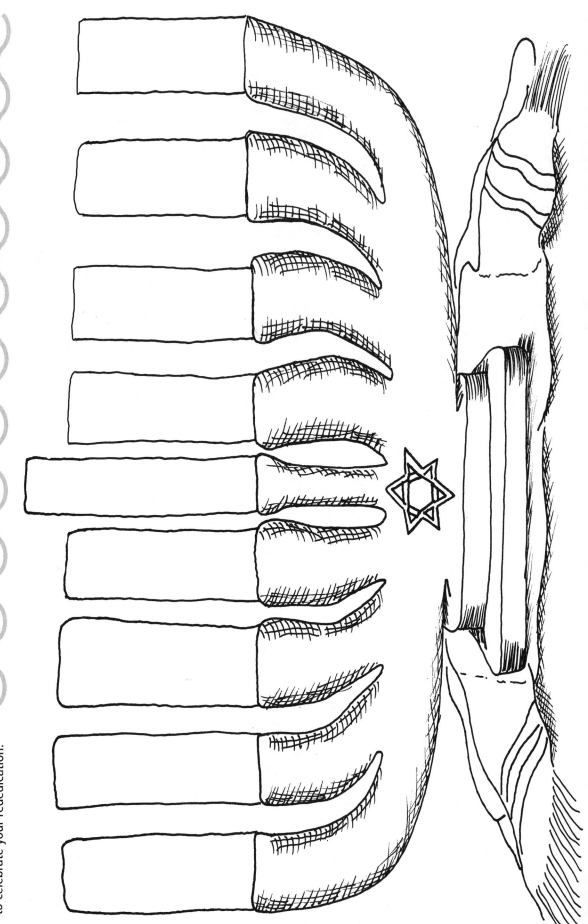

Paper Dreidel

Create your own paper dreidel and then play the game.

Materials

paper
pencil
crayons
scissors
glue

1. Color the dreidel and write your name on it.

2. Cut out the dreidel.

3. Carefully poke a small hole through the circle at the top and bottom (just start the hole, you will poke the pencil all the way through later).

4. Fold along the lines.

5. Glue tabs.

6. Carefully poke the pencil all the way through to finish your dreidel.

How to Play

1. Players start with 10–15 coins, candies, chips, etc.

2. Each player puts one into the "pot" to start.

3. Players then decide how many they will add each turn.

4. A player spins the dreidel and follows the action of the letter on the side that landed up.

5. Players take turns spinning until one player wins all.

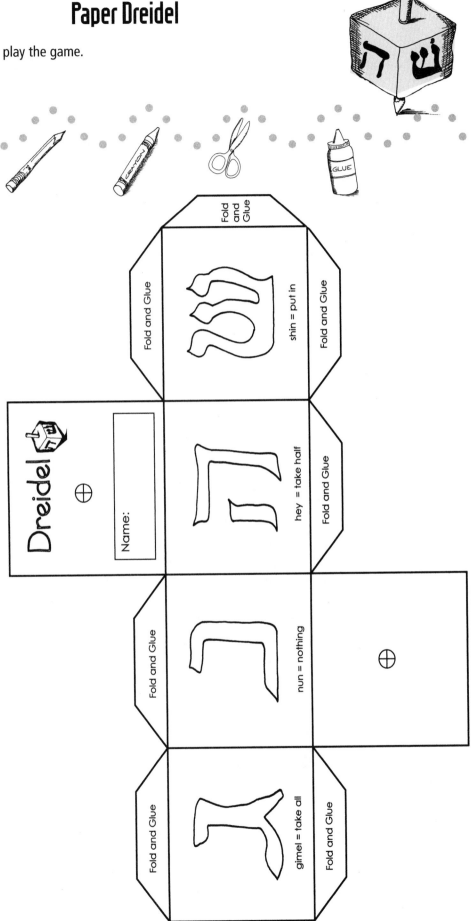

Dreidel

Name:

Fold and Glue

shin = put in

hey = take half

nun = nothing

gimel = take all

Hanukkah Teacher Resource Page

Title

Colorful Border

Student Question

Teacher Example

Children's Work

Rubric Score/
Teacher Feedback

Rubric

State Standard

What eight things will you work to improve on in school.

9.9 State standard that refers to this activity.

Lesson Extensions

- Create a Rededication bulletin board. Display menorah pages.
- Make latkes (potato pancakes).
- Do a research report or Venn diagram comparing the similarities and differences between Hanukkah and Christmas and Hanukkah and Kwanzaa.
- Make edible menorahs. Use a graham cracker as the base. Marshmallows can be the candles with a larger marshmallow in the middle. Attach with frosting.

Word Bank

Hanukkah
Jewish
Hebrew
temple
lamp
menorah
dreidel
latke
gelt
oil

Children's Literature Ideas

Use for read-alouds, shared reading, silent reading, research, and so on.

Heiligman, D. (2006). *Celebrate Hanukkah with Light, Latkes, and Dreidels.* National Geographic Society. ISBN: 0792259246.

Johnston, M. C. (2002). *Hanukkah.* The Children's World. ISBN: 156766024X.

Krensky, H. (2006). *Hanukkah at Valley Forge.* Penguin. ISBN: 0525477381.

Rosen, M. (2006). *Chanukah Lights Everywhere.* Globe Pequot Press. ISBN: 0152056750.

Schotter, R. (2003). *Hanukkah!* Little, Brown and Co. ISBN: 0316776238.

Christmas

What is the first thing you think of when someone mentions Christmas? Gifts? Food? Trees? Decorations? Most likely you consider Santa Claus, carols, wreaths, lights, church, and family, too. You may have a feeling of warmth mixed with excitement. This is the time of year when people get together with family and friends to share the thrill of Santa Claus and giving gifts, and Christians celebrate the birth of Jesus Christ.

The birthday of Jesus was initially celebrated on January 6, the feast of Epiphany, a feast honoring the deity of Christ. In A.D. 354, the date was changed to December 25. Christians used this new date to replace several pagan festivals and traditions of the season. These festivals were popular because workloads were lighter after the fall harvest, and the festivals carried into the winter season. In ancient Babylon and Egypt, a mid-winter festival celebrated the birth of the ancient sun-god Attis in Phrygia on December 25, as well as the birth of the Persian sun-god, Mithras. The Roman god of peace and plenty, Saturn, was celebrated in the festival Saturnalia, December 17–24, with the winter solstice on December 21. In Scandinavia, a time of festivities known as Yule was celebrated. It was a time to enjoy the harvests

267

of summer with much feasting and cheerfulness. Christmas took the place of these celebrations and rituals.

Although the festivals may have been replaced, some of the traditions remained and became Christmas traditions despite their pagan roots. One such tradition, which has its early roots in the Celtic culture, is mistletoe and holly. The Celtic culture respected nature and all green plants. Two such highly regarded plants were mistletoe and holly, believed to be important symbols of fertility. This traditional Christmas greenery was used for decorating homes and altars.

Through the years new traditions continued to be added to Christmas. Carols became attached to Christmas in the 14th century. The nativity, the re-enactment of the manger scene where Jesus was said to be born, was started by St. Francis to increase the spiritual knowledge of the Italian people. St. Nicholas, honored on December 6 for centuries, helped to create our Santa Claus. Even the yule log can be traced to pagan traditions. All of these traditions have come to form our modern traditions of Christmas.

Christmas has become a magical time of flying reindeers and visits from Santa. Many children write letters with their gift wish lists or even visit Santa to sit on his lap and share their lists. Those who celebrate know that Rudolph with his shiny red nose will lead Santa's sleigh from the North Pole as he circumnavigates the globe to deliver presents to all the good boys and girls of the world. Many children leave cookies or a snack for Santa to help him through his long journey. According to tradition, he slides down chimneys with his bag of toys, all made by elves in his North Pole workshop. Then he places gifts under Christmas trees and fills children's stockings with them. For those who celebrate, Christmas creates lifetime memories and still brings the child out in everyone.

The actually celebration of Christmas has always stirred some controversy. It is so different from the simple roots of the nativity that it celebrates. Through time the holiday has grown and become very commercialized. Some say the true meaning of Christmas has been lost.

Regardless, today, Christmas is still an annual day that celebrates the birth of Jesus. While the precise chronology of Jesus' birth and death is still debated, the holiday is traditionally observed on December 25. Christmas has many aspects, both religious and secular, including the exchange of gifts, Santa Claus, stories of elves and reindeer, the decoration and display of Christmas trees, and religious ceremonies. Either way, remember that Christmas is not just a time to receive, but more important, a time to give.

Name: _____   Date: _____

Word Bank

Santa Claus	reindeer	mistletoe	stocking	chimney
lights	wreath	presents	tree	snowman

Illustrate these four words:

The tree has 26 Christmas bulbs. 9 of the bulbs fell off and broke. How many bulbs are left on the tree?

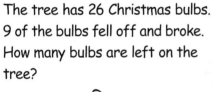

Which one of these people is said to deliver gifts to good boys and girls? Circle that person.

Make a list of all the things you would like to get for Christmas.

Decorate the snowman.

Name: _____   Date: _____

Word Bank					
	Santa Claus	reindeer	mistletoe	stocking	chimney
	lights	wreath	presents	tree	snowman

Illustrate these four words:

stocking	_chimney_	_wreath_	_reindeer_

There are 400 lights on the Christmas tree. 342 of the lights are red. What percent of the lights are red?

Which one of these items does *not* come from trees? Cross it out.

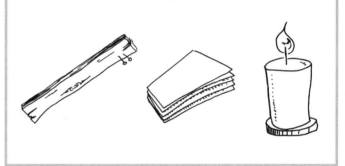

Draw the other half of Santa Claus.

Make an outline for a note you want to write Santa Claus about the cookies you have left for him.

Name:

Date:

Merry Christmas and Happy New Year!

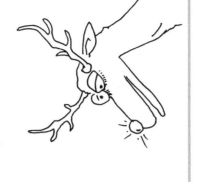

Write about how you celebrate Christmas.

Name: _____   Date: _____

Christmas Wreath Journal: Write about what Christmas means to you.

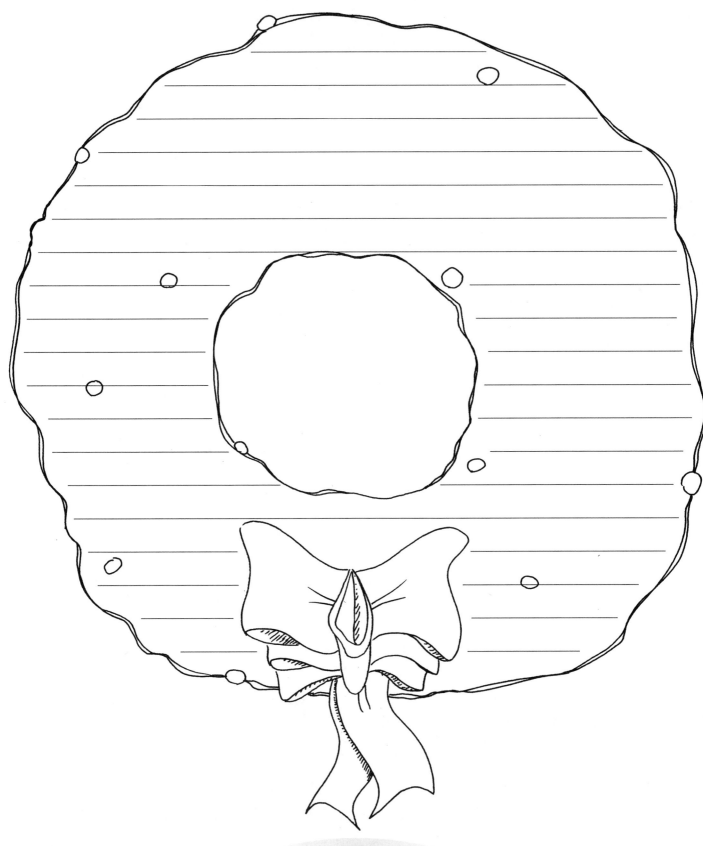

Christmas Stocking

Students can make their own Christmas stockings. • • • • • • • • • • • • • • • •

Materials

red construction paper
stapler
hole punch
yarn
ribbon
glue
cotton
crayons
glitter

1. Start by making two copies of the stocking on red construction paper for each student.

2. Have students decorate the opposite sides of each stocking.

3. Students should cut out both of their stockings.

4. You can decide whether you want to staple the stocking together or use the hole punch and sew the sides together with yarn. Connect the stocking all around the edge, leaving the top open.

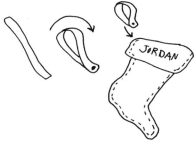

5. Have students make a loop with ribbon or paper to use for hanging the stocking.

6. Students can glue small pieces of cotton on the top of the stocking.

7. When finished, fill with candy and hang them in the room. You can also stuff the stockings with paper instead of candy and seal the top.

273

Christmas Stocking Template

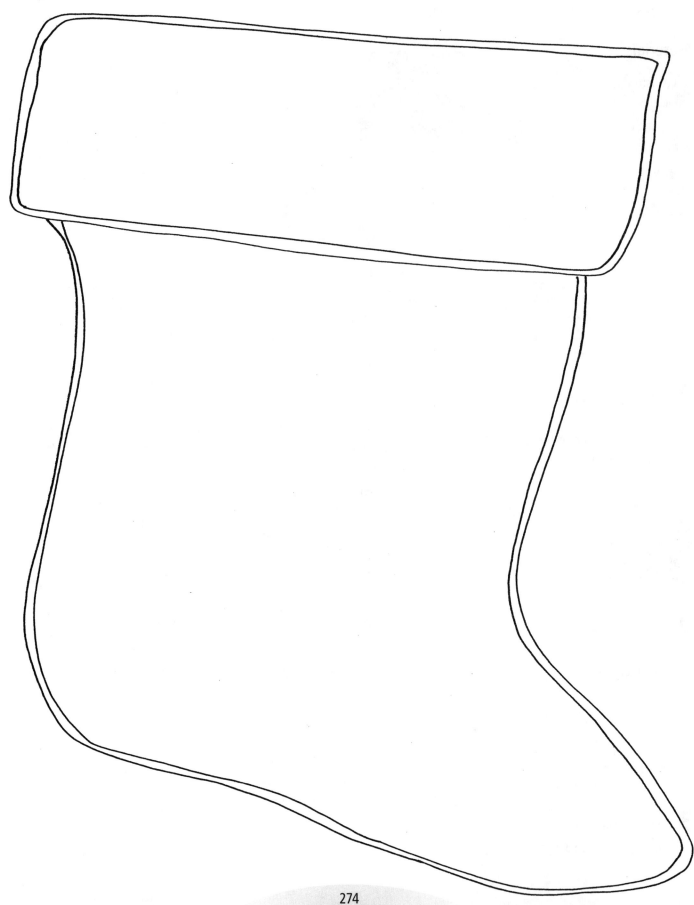

Hand Wreath

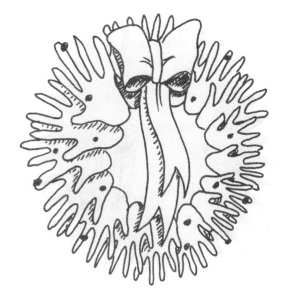

Materials

green construction paper
ribbon
glue
scissors
red scrap paper or red buttons
pencil

1. Begin by having students trace their hands, making about 10 copies. (More hands are required for a larger wreath.)

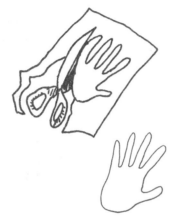

2. Have students cut out all of their hands and glue them together in a circle, forming the body of the wreath.

3. When the wreath is finished, let the glue dry. Students can then begin to decorate. Use ribbon to make a bow and red scrap paper for the berries, or try using an assortment of red buttons instead.

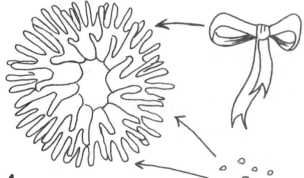

4. Hang the wreaths in the classroom or send them home for students to hang on their front doors.

MERRY CHRISTMAS!

Hand-Foot Reindeer

crayons
scissors
glue
pencil
brown paper
Popsicle stick
red paper

1. Have each student trace his or her hand twice and foot once on brown paper. They then cut out all three pieces.

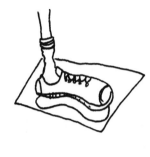

2. Students glue the three pieces together, adding three small ovals (two eyes and one nose).

3. Students can decorate with crayons and glue the reindeer to a paper bag or mount on a Popsicle stick!

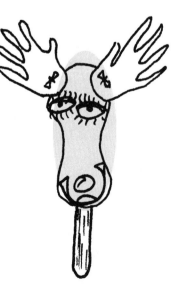

Christmas Teacher Resource Page

Title

Colorful Border

Student Question

Teacher Example

Children's Work

Rubric Score/Teacher Feedback

Rubric

State Standard

Christmas Gift List

What are the presents on your Christmas list?

1.4 State standard that refers to this lesson.

RUBRIC
4
3
2
1

Lesson Extensions

- Create a Christmas bulletin board.
- Have a gift exchange (Secret Santa) for those who participate in Christmas. Remember to always have extra gifts on hand for those who forgot to bring one.
- Create and fill Christmas stockings before the winter break.
- Learn Christmas songs/carols and go caroling to other classrooms.
- Make Christmas cards.

Word Bank

Santa Claus
lights
reindeer
wreath
mistletoe
presents
stocking
tree
chimney
snowman

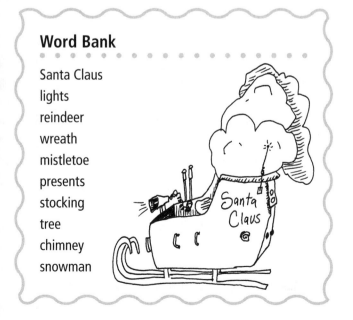

Children's Literature Ideas

Use for read-alouds, shared reading, silent reading, research, and so on.

DePaola, T. (2006). *Christmas Remembered.* Penguin. ISBN: 0399246223.

Dickens, C. (1990). *A Christmas Carol.* Tor Books Publishing. ISBN: 0812504348.

Moore, C. (2002). *The Night Before Christmas.* Michael Friedman Publishing Group. ISBN: 076073397X.

Pfister, M. (2004). *The Christmas Star.* North-South Books. ISBN: 0735819734.

Pingry, P. (1998). *The Story of Christmas.* Ideals Publications. ISBN: 0824940911.

Boxing Day

In many countries, Boxing Day is celebrated each year on December 26, the day after Christmas. It is an official government holiday in Australia, Great Britain, New Zealand, and Canada. On this day family and friends come together for good food and good times. It is also a very busy shopping day—malls and stores stay open offering special sales and Christmas exchanges. In Canada, it is the biggest shopping day of the year.

But shopping is only a very small part of Boxing Day. It is actually a very special day set aside to give to the less fortunate. It is believed to have been started centuries ago in the Middle Ages and became officially estab-

lished in England under Queen Victoria. Members of the merchant class would gather food, clothing, and other necessities for servants and tradespeople as their way of saying thanks. All these gifts were placed in boxes, giving the holiday its name.

Another version involves the wealthier classes giving gift boxes to their servants on that day since the servants had to work on Christmas itself. These servants also received as their reward a day off to spend with their own families.

Another influence or possible origin of this holiday has to do with the churches. Churches opened their Christmas alms donation boxes each year on the day after Christmas, the Feast of St. Stephen's Day, to give to the poor and needy. St. Stephen believed in helping widows and the poor.

Regardless of the holiday's exact origins, it is a very special day to give and appreciate all we have in our own lives and those who have helped us, such as a postal carrier or gardener. In addition, families, businesses, and organizations may donate more than just gift boxes. Many also donate their time and volunteer services and money to worthy causes for the less fortunate.

This day of giving is a great tradition to follow Christmas. The holidays are a time to give and receive, but that can be hard on those who cannot provide for their families. Celebrating Boxing Day is a way to reach out, reflect, and be filled with gratitude. It is a time to think of how we can help the needy. Collections of canned goods, clothes, and other necessities can be placed in boxes and given to agencies that assist those in need.

Name: _____ **Date:** _____

| fortunate | food | poor | give | gratitude |
| box | clothing | needy | donate | volunteer |

Illustrate these four words:

box	donate	food	clothing

Room 27 collected cans of food for Boxing Day. Alexis brought 4, Cynthia brought 6, and Zach brought 5. How many cans did they have in all?

Circle and color the items that would be good for a gift box and put an X over those that would not be good.

Gratitude List
_____

Gratitude means "being thankful." You can be thankful for your parents, friends, or even chocolate milk. Just be thankful. List three things that you are thankful for in your life.

1. _____

_____

2. _____

_____

3. _____

_____

Draw what you would put in a gift box on Boxing Day.

Name: _____ Date: _____

| fortunate | food | poor | give | gratitude |
| box | clothing | needy | donate | volunteer |

Illustrate these four words:

donate

food

box

clothing

Room 18 made a gift box for Boxing Day. Karen brought 7 canned goods, Luis brought 4 boxes of cereal, and James brought 9 shirts. They had 20 items in all. Calculate the percent each item was of all the items.

7 cans = _____%

4 boxes = _____%

9 shirts = _____%
_____
20 items

Boxing Day Trivia
_____

Boxing Day originated in _____.

_____ is the patron saint who believed in helping widows and the poor. This is the saint that has the same day as Boxing Day. Boxing Day occurs on _____ each year.

Gratitude means "being thankful." You can be thankful for your parents, friends, or even chocolate milk. Just be thankful! List three things you are thankful for in your life.

1. _____

_____

2. _____

_____

3. _____

_____

What would you include in your gift box for Boxing Day?

Name: _____

Date: _____

Write about Boxing Day. What would you add to your gift box? Illustrate.

_____

_____

_____

_____

Word Bank   fortunate   box   food   clothing   poor   needy   give   donate   gratitude   volunteer

Name: _____ Date: _____

Write about Boxing Day. What would you add to your gift box? Illustrate.

_____
_____
_____
_____
_____
_____
_____
_____
_____
_____
_____
_____
_____
_____

Word Bank   fortunate   box   food   clothing   poor   needy   give   donate   gratitude   volunteer

Penny Donation Box

In honor of Boxing Day create a donation box of your own. You can collect pennies and then donate them to your favorite charity. Little by little, the pennies will add up to a nice amount.

Materials

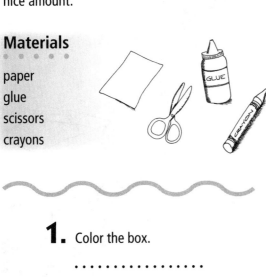

paper
glue
scissors
crayons

1. Color the box.

. . . .

2. Cut out the box.

. . . .

3. Fold tabs and box sides.

. . . .

4. Glue flaps.

. . . .

5. Collect pennies.

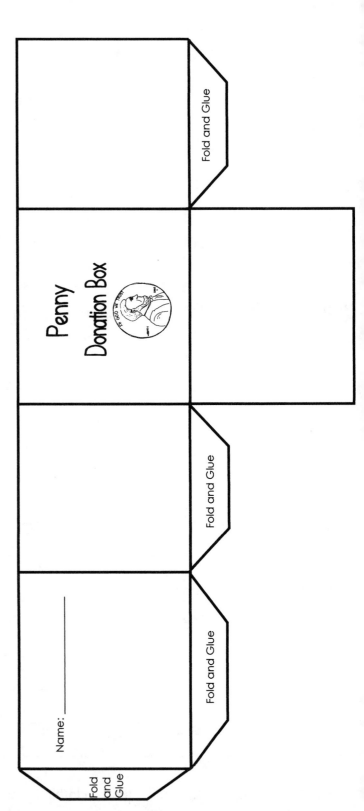

Fold and Glue

Penny Donation Box

Fold and Glue

Fold and Glue

Name: _____

Fold and Glue

Thank-You Card

Being grateful is important, and one way to show our gratitude is to thank those who have helped us. Boxing Day is a wonderful chance to think of others, but we don't have to have a special day to do this. We can thank others every day with a smile, a flower, or even a simple "Thanks."

Use this template to make thank-you cards for someone you are grateful for. As a class you can pick people from around the school. A secretary, a cafeteria worker, a bus driver are all people who help. Create cards to say thanks.

Just color, decorate, cut out, and fold. Enjoy showing someone your gratitude!

Thank-you!

Dear _____

Boxing Day Teacher Resource Page

Title

Colorful Border

Student Question

Teacher Example

Children's Work

Rubric Score/ Teacher Feedback

Rubric

State Standard

What items can help make someone's life a little better?

3.5 State standard that refers to this activity.

Lesson Extensions

- Create a Donation bulletin board.
- Collect donations for a box to be given to someone in need.
- Contact various volunteer organizations and invite them to visit the classroom.
- Volunteer to help out around the school.
- Save change and give it to a favorite charity.

Word Bank

fortunate
box
food
clothing
poor
needy
give
donate
gratitude
volunteer

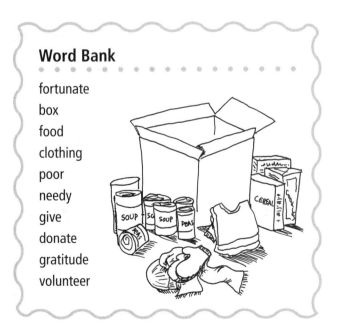

Children's Literature Ideas

Use for read-alouds, shared reading, silent reading, research, and so on.

Andersen, H. C. (2002). *The Little Match Girl.* Penguin. ISBN: 0142301884.

Baylor, S. (1998). *The Table Where Rich People Sit.* Simon & Schuster. ISBN: 0689820089.

Bunting, E. (1989). *The Wednesday Surprise.* Houghton Mifflin. ISBN: 0395547768.

Chinn, K. (1997). *Sam and the Lucky Money.* Lee & Low Books. ISBN: 1880000539.

Hess-Pomeranc, M. (1998). *The Can-do Thanksgiving.* Albert Whitman Publishers. ISBN: 0807510548.

Kwanzaa

Kwanzaa is a seven-day African American holiday celebrated from December 26 to January 1 each year. A cultural rather than a religious holiday, it is not intended to replace Christmas. The holiday is meant to inspire African Americans to have greater pride in their heritage. Dr. Maulana "Ron" Karenga, a professor of Black Studies, created Kwanzaa in 1966. The 1960s were a time of cultural revolution for African Americans, and Kwanzaa was designed to celebrate and honor the values of ancient African cultures.

Kwanzaa is based on the year-end harvest festivals of Africa that have been celebrated for thousands of years. This holiday builds on an ancient and living cultural tradition reflecting the best of African thought and practice. It ties together the dignity, well-being, environment, and culture of the individual and the community.

The name *Kwanzaa* comes from the Swahili phrase *matunda ya kwanza*, which translates to "first fruits of the harvest." For the holiday an extra *a* was added to make the word *Kwanzaa*, giving it seven letters—one letter for each of the seven principles. Kwanzaa is a unique holiday because people of all religions can celebrate it since it is not recognized as a religious holiday. It is all about family and community, and so far hasn't become as commercialized as some other holidays have.

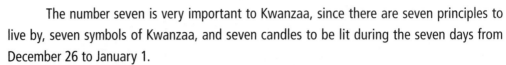

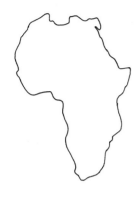

The number seven is very important to Kwanzaa, since there are seven principles to live by, seven symbols of Kwanzaa, and seven candles to be lit during the seven days from December 26 to January 1.

The principles of Kwanzaa are the key to the celebration. They help build strong, productive families and communities. People greet one another with the expression, "*Habari gani*" ("What's the news?"), which the principles of Kwanzaa address.

- The first principle (December 26) is *Umoja*, which stands for unity and has a black candle.
- The second principle (December 27) is *Kujichagulia*, which stands for self-determination and has a red candle.
- The third principle (December 28) is *Ujima*, which stands for collective work and responsibility and has a green candle.
- The fourth principle (December 29) is *Ujamaa*, which stands for cooperative economics and helping to build strong financial foundations and has a red candle.
- The fifth principle (December 30) is *Nia*, which stands for the reinvigoration of our sense of purpose and has a green candle.
- The sixth principle (December 31) is *Kuumba*, which stands for creativity where African arts take center stage and has a red candle.

- The seventh principle (January 1) is *Imani*, which stands for faith and has a green candle. A wonderful feast, *Karamu*, is served and homemade gifts, *zawadi*, are shared.

The candles, called *Mishumaa Saba*, are placed on a candelabrum, called a *Kinara*. Each night of Kwanzaa the candles are lit and its principle is discussed. There are one black, three red, and three green candles, all of which have special significance. The black candle represents the rich color of African American skin. The red candles symbolize the struggles of their people, and the green candles symbolize hope for a prosperous future. The candles are lit each night in alternating colors, working from the inside out. After the first black candle is lit on the first night, the red candle closest to the black one is lit for the second night. The third night the innermost green candle is lit, and so on.

Kwanzaa is a holiday full of symbols. A special straw mat called a *Mkeka* is where the Kinara is placed. Ears of corn, *Vibunzi,* one for each child of the house, are also placed on the Mkeka. A fruit basket, a *Mazao*, is also placed on the Mkeka along with the unity cup called *Kikombe cha umoja.*

There are two major events that take place during Kwanzaa. One is the feast of Karamu, in which cultural expression is celebrated in order to bring people closer to their African roots. It is a great feast with traditional African dishes made with ingredients that originate in Africa. The other is Imani, the last day of Kwanzaa. This is a day that honors traditions and one's self-worth through gift-giving. All the gifts are handmade, which supports the principle of creativity, Kuumba.

Celebrating Kwanzaa is not only a cultural experience for all, but one of great empowerment for the people this holiday represents.

Name: _____   Date: _____

Word Bank				
corn	candle	place mat	Africa	gifts
cup	fruit	Kinara	family	celebration

Illustrate these four words:

 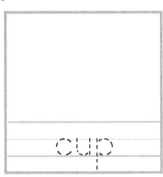  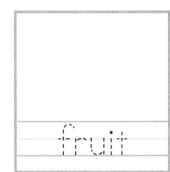

corn   cup   candle   fruit

Write a subtraction problem that goes with the picture of the Kinara.

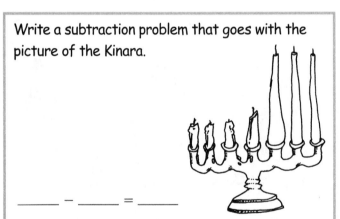

_____ – _____ = _____

Circle the item you would find at a Kwanzaa celebration.

Draw and color the candles on the Kwanzaa Kinara.

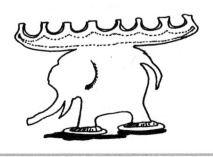

Draw ears of corn on the Kwanzaa mat to represent each of the children in your family, including yourself.

Word Bank	corn	candle	place mat	Africa	gifts
	cup	fruit	Kinara	family	celebration

Illustrate these four words:

Kinara	*Africa*	*place mat*	*fruit*

21 students each have a Kinara in Mr. Burnett's class. How many candles will the teacher need for the students? 2 more students come to class late. How many candles will the teacher need now?

Which item would you find on the Kwanzaa mat? Circle it.

Draw the other six symbols of Kwanzaa on the mat below.

Fill in the bubbles with words that describe what you are thankful for.

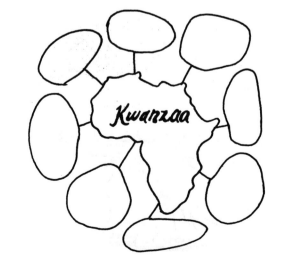

Kwanzaa

Name: _____

Date: _____

Write about the Kinara and draw the other five items that go with it for a super Kwanzaa celebration! Be sure to color your picture.

Describe what you do to celebrate cultural traditions in your family.

Kwanzaa Kinara

For a fun activity, your students can make a Kinara out of paper for their desks.

1. Start by coloring the candles and the Kinara.

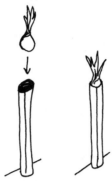

2. After coloring, cut out all the pieces of the Kinara.

10. Push each kernel down into the candles. (Make sure the glue is dry!) The candles are finished, and students now have a Kinara to enjoy during the Kwanzaa celebration.

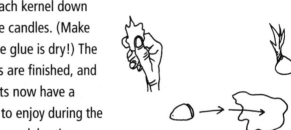

9. Take small pieces of red tissue paper and wrap them around kernels of popcorn. (These will be the flames on the candles.)

3. Fold and glue the Kinara. Let it dry.

4. Place two pennies inside to add a little weight.

8. Put a drop of glue at the base of each candle to keep them in place.

5. Use a pencil or scissors to poke the holes for the candles to fit in.

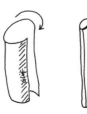

6. Roll and glue the candles. Let them dry.

7. Push all the candles into their holes.

Kwanzaa Kinara

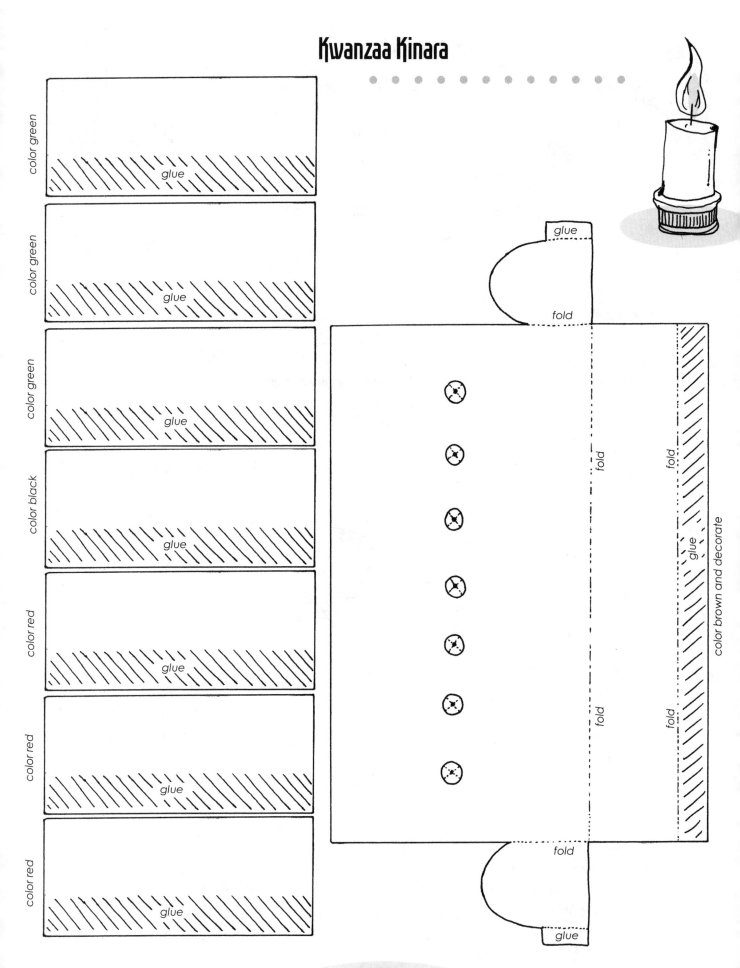

color green

glue

color green

glue

color green

glue

color black

glue

color red

glue

color red

glue

color red

glue

glue

fold

fold

fold

fold

glue

color brown and decorate

fold

glue

Celebration Mat

The celebration mat is a very important part of Kwanzaa. Students can make their own and share its importance with their families.

Materials

paper (red, black, green)
pencil
ruler
scissors
glue

1. Using the ruler, make straight lines running horizontally across the paper about an inch apart.

2. Cut each line going across the paper, but stop short at the end, keeping the strips connected.

3. Cut the other two color papers into strips about an inch wide.

4. Begin weaving one of the strips over and under the original sheet that was cut.

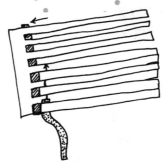

5. After the first sheet is through, alternate colors weaving the second strip. Continue weaving the other strips until the mat is full.

6. Trim and glue all the ends.

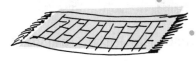

7. When finished, take home or create a Kwanzaa table setting.

Kwanza Flag with Corn

Materials

paper (red, black, green)
glue
scissors
popcorn
pencil

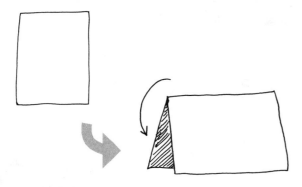

1. Fold the red sheet of paper in half.

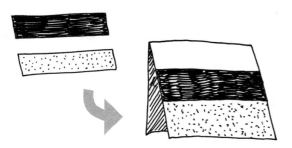

2. Cut and glue a strip of black for the middle and green for the bottom. Strips should be of equal size.

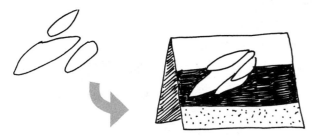

3. Cut and glue oval shapes of light green paper. One is the large ear of corn, and the smaller pieces are the husks.

4. Glue the kernels of popcorn on the main ear of corn as decoration.

5. Write a message inside and share!

Kwanzaa Teacher Resource Page

Title

Colorful Border

Student Question

Teacher Example

Children's Work

Rubric Score/
Teacher Feedback

Rubric

State Standard

How many siblings are in your family?

1.4 State standard that refers to this lesson.

Muhindi (The Corn)
London

Rubric
4
3
2
1

Lesson Extensions

- Have students make ears of corn representing themselves. Create a class Kwanzaa place setting on a bulletin board.
- Invite a community member in to speak about Kwanzaa.
- An important aspect of Kwanzaa is the theme of reading books and their importance. Have a classroom book exchange. Students can bring in books to exchange with other students.
- Create an actual Kwanzaa setting on a desk using realia.
- Have students learn and recite a Kwanzaa poem for a culminating activity.

Word Bank

corn
cup
candle
fruit
place mat
Kinara
Africa
family
gifts
celebration

Children's Literature Ideas

Use for read-alouds, shared reading, silent reading, research, and so on.

Ford, J. (2003). *K Is for Kwanzaa.* Scholastic, Inc. ISBN: 0439560713.

Ford, J. (2000). *Together for Kwanzaa.* Random House Children's Books. ISBN: 0375803297.

Medearis, A. (2006). *Seven Spools of Thread: A Kwanzaa Story.* Albert Whitman. ISBN: 0807573167.

Murray, J. (2003) *Kwanzaa.* ABDO Publishing. ISBN: 1577659554.

Robertson, L. (2003). *Kwanzaa Fun: Great Things to Make and Do.* Houghton Mifflin. ISBN: 0753456850.

New Year's Eve and Day

The first day of a calendar year, January 1, was introduced as New Year's Day in the 1500s when Pope Gregory announced modifications to the Julian calendar system and reset the first day of the year from April 1 to January 1. This calendar, named the Gregorian calendar, is used by most of the world today. The word *January* comes from the Roman god, Janus, who was the god of gates and doors, beginnings and endings. Janus had two faces, one that looked forward to the new year and the other that looked backward at the past year.

New Year's Day is celebrated around the world, as most countries use the same calendar system. The calendar is solar-based, marking the complete orbit of the Earth around the sun. People traditionally begin to celebrate the night before, on New Year's Eve, with parties and countdowns to midnight. A champagne toast has become common among adults, and parties are filled with party hats, noisemakers, and confetti—all to celebrate and make noise welcoming the New Year. This is also a time to reflect on the year gone by and to make resolutions for the year to come.

In the United States, one of the most famous celebrations takes place in Times Square in New York City. Crowds gather at this landmark location to watch as a giant ball slowly drops seconds before midnight and then lights up as it hits the bottom and the clock strikes midnight.

Name: _____   **Date:** _____

Word Bank

| January | Janus | midnight | hat | confetti |
| eve | calendar | resolution | party | horn |

Illustrate these four words:

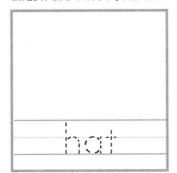 hat	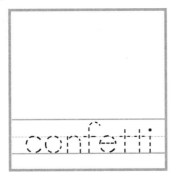 confetti	 horn	 party

---

Kimberly and Michael had a New Year's Eve party. They gave out 12 hats, 11 noisemakers, and 6 horns. How many items did they give out in all?

_____

_____

_____

Circle the party favors that make noise. Underline the party favor you wear. Make an X on the party favors you have to blow into.

Draw yourself at the New Year's Eve party.

Calendar Trivia _____

There are:

_____ days in a year.

_____ months in a year.

_____ days in a week.

_____ days in January.

My birthday is _____.

Name: _____ Date: _____

Illustrate these four words:

Janus	*confetti*	*calendar*	*eve*

At the New Year's Eve party there were 100 party favors. Write the percent and fraction that represents each type of party favor.

30   35   20   15

Calendar Trivia

There are _____ days in one year.

There are _____ months in a year.

There are _____ days in a week.

There are _____ weeks in a year.

_____ is the shortest month.

_____ is my birthday.

New Year is a time for resolutions. Write three things that you want to work on this next year.

1. _____

_____

2. _____

_____

3. _____

_____

Draw yourself and a friend at the New Year's Eve party.

Name: _____

Date: _____

Write about how you celebrate New Year's
Eve and New Year's Day. Illustrate.

_____

_____

_____

_____

Word Bank   January   eve   Janus   calendar   midnight   resolution   hat   party   confetti   horn

Name: _____   Date: _____

Write about how you celebrate New Year's Eve and New Year's Day. Illustrate.

_____
_____
_____
_____

_____
_____
_____
_____
_____
_____
_____
_____

Word Bank   January   eve   Janus   calendar   midnight   resolution   hat   party   confetti   horn

Name: _____ Date: _____

New Year's Day Resolution Letter: Write a New Year's resolution letter to your parents describing your goals for the coming year.

January ____, _____

Dear _____,

_____

_____

_____

_____

_____

_____

_____

_____

_____

_____

_____

_____

_____

_____

Sincerely yours,

_____

Word Bank   try   improve   learn   promise   goal   accomplish   progress

New Year's Day Teacher Resource Page

Title

Colorful Border

Student Question

Teacher Example

Children's Work

Rubric Score/Teacher Feedback

Rubric

State Standard

What are your New Year's resolutions?

2.8 State standard that refers to this activity.

Lesson Extensions

- Write out resolutions (see the New Year's Day Resolution Letter activity) and create a New Year's Resolution bulletin board.
- Make party hats and confetti to take home for holiday celebrations.
- Create personal time lines. Students can represent each year with a self-portrait or a description or illustration of a significant event in their lives.

Word Bank

January
eve
Janus
calendar
midnight
resolution
hat
party
confetti
horn

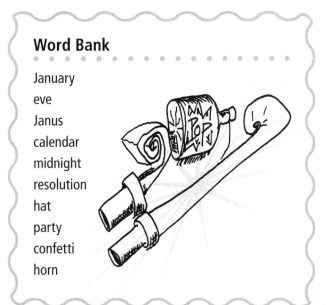

Children's Literature Ideas

Use for read-alouds, shared reading, silent reading, research, and so on.

Lewis, P. (1999). *Polar Bear's New Year's Party: A Counting Book*. Ten Speed Press. ISBN: 1883672996.

Martin, B. (1992). *The Happy Hippopotami*. Harcourt. ISBN: 0152333827.

Marx, D. (2000). *New Year's Day*. Scholastic Library Publishers. ISBN: 0516271563.

Ruelle, K. (2004). *Just in Time for New Year's: A Harry and Emily Adventure*. Holiday House, Inc. ISBN: 0823418421.

Bibliography

The following websites were used to fact-check the historical and cultural facts information used in this book. However, these websites are also great tools for teachers to obtain more extensive information to share with their students or to encourage students to visit when researching the holidays.

. . . .

apples4theteacher.com/holidays/new-years-day/
index.html#aboutnewyears

arborday.org/arborday/history.cfm

calendar-updates.com/info/holidays/canada/
boxing.aspx

canadianhistory.suite101.com/article.cfm/
victoria_day

christmas-time.com/cp-hist.html

cs.uiowa.edu/~jones/voting/pictures

dol.gov/opa/aboutdol/laborday.htm

educationworld.com/a_lesson/00-2/lp2257.shtml

en.wikipedia.org

enchantedlearning.com

factmonster.com

flaglerelections.com/kids/history.htm

holidays.net

holidayspotplus.com/holiday_int_canadian
_victoria.htm

homeschooling.about.com/cs/unitssubjhol/a/
cincodemayo.htm

infoplease.com/spot/mayday.html

inventors.about.com/library/weekly/aa111300b.htm

kumc.edu/diversity/other/valentin.html

latino.sscnet.ucla.edu/demo/cinco.html

loggia.com/myth/cupid.html

meridiangraphics.net/lupercalia.htm

mexonline.com/cinco.htm

museumofhoaxes.com/aforigin.html

new-life.net/thanks01.htm

pbskids.org/democracy

pch.gc.ca/progs/cpsc-ccsp/jfa-ha/canada_e.cfm

public.iastate.edu/~rjsalvad/scmfaq/muertos.html

stockholm.usembassy.gov/Holidays/celebrate

submission.org

usacitylink.com/usa

usemb.se/Holidays

usembassyjakarta.org/columbus.html

veteransagency.mod.uk/veteransday/index.htm

wilstar.com/holidays

youthonline.ca/boxingday